Contents

Robin Small

Karl Marx

The Revolutionary as Educator

Robin Small
The University of Auckland
Auckland
New Zealand

ISSN 2211-937X ISSN 2211-9388 (electronic)
ISBN 978-94-007-7656-2 ISBN 978-94-007-7657-9 (eBook)
DOI 10.1007/978-94-007-7657-9
Springer Dordrecht Heidelberg New York London

Library of Congress Control Number: 2013948864

Printed on acid-free paper

Springer is part of Springer Science+Business Media (www.springer.com)

Chapter 1
The Education of an Educator

Abstract Marx received an academic schooling in his native Rhineland, based on classical studies and strongly influenced by Enlightenment thinkers such as Immanuel Kant. At Berlin University, he mixed with the radically minded younger Hegelians who followed Ludwig Feuerbach's call to engage with the world of experience and feeling. Even so, the dominating influence of Hegelian idealism is evident in Marx's 1841 doctoral dissertation, a study of ancient materialism. His first career as a newspaper editor is marked by outspoken opposition to censorship and government paternalism. Following his teachers, he champions individual freedom of thought and speech. But Marx grows disillusioned with liberalism as he comes to see the reforms needed for realising its goals as impossible within the present social system. In debate with his former mentor Bruno Bauer over Jewish emancipation, he argues that theological criticism must be replaced by social criticism, since the real problems are those of an economic system that runs on self-interest.

Keywords Karl Marx • Education • Enlightenment • Bildung • Liberalism

1.1 Introduction

Karl Marx is an important educational thinker. This may come as a surprise to anyone who looks at standard surveys of philosophy of education. Well-known figures in the Western tradition appear there, starting with Plato and Aristotle, and including modern figures such as Locke, Rousseau and Dewey. Marx is usually left out. Yet amongst thinkers on education, Marx is especially relevant to the twenty-first century. He is the greatest theorist of the society that gave rise to schools as we know them—and this is the society we still live in. So what Marx has to say about the place of education in the modern world should be worth attention.

R. Small, *Karl Marx*, SpringerBriefs on Key Thinkers in Education,
DOI: 10.1007/978-94-007-7657-9_1, © The Author(s) 2014

But Marx is not just a theorist. He is a revolutionary, committed to transforming the world. In his words, 'The philosophers have only interpreted the world in various ways; the point, however, is to change it' (Marx and Engels 1975–2005, vol. 5, p. 8). This does not mean *replacing* interpretation with changing the world, though. Marx has little time for what he calls 'that kind of criticism which knows how to judge and condemn the present, but not how to comprehend it' (Marx and Engels 1975–2005, vol. 35, p. 507). He is saying that the point of interpreting the world is to change it. In other words, he wants both understanding and engagement. But how do we make the link between theory and practice? Marx's idea of 'praxis' provides a clue, but his full answer depends on developing an approach which exposes ideological modes of thought as both false and acting to maintain an unjust social reality. Marx's main writings are not just analyses but critiques, designed to undermine conventional wisdom and point the way to something better.

This means that Marx is himself an educator. He writes for people who need to find out what is wrong with the society they live in and how it can be changed for the better. Given that aim, it would be surprising if he had nothing to say about an important aspect of modern society: its arrangements for its own new members. It is true that Marx was never an academic teacher or researcher, but this goes for other important figures in education. It is also true that he did not write any works solely on education. Yet he wrote more on the subject than most people think (Small 2005). His concern was society as a whole, and whatever he says about education tends to be part of some wider discussion. Still, these texts contain enough to provide not just an understanding of the schooling of his time but also a surprisingly detailed plan for the schooling of the future.

Most importantly, Marx is an educator for us. He challenges us to develop our capacity to think critically about our own society and, in particular, to look beneath the surface of schooling and find out what is really happening in this area of social life. This book approaches Marx's contributions by following the course of his intellectual career within its historical context. It deals in turn with his early thought as an expression of the turbulent 1840s, the politically static period during which he set out on a full analysis of the capitalist mode of production, and his later re-emergence on the political stage. As we shall see, Marx's thinking about education is present throughout his career, varying in its focus according to the tasks of the time but broadly consistent in its direction. A closer look will reveal some unfamiliar ideas—and even some surprises.

To understand Karl Marx, it helps to know about the Rhineland, his place of origin. Marx was born in Trier, an ancient city just within the border of the Roman Empire. Visitors can still see evidence of its past: an amphitheatre and public baths, as well as the Porta Nigra, one of the most impressive city gates still standing. In the fifth century Trier was the birthplace of St Ambrose, later bishop of Milan and mentor of St Augustine. After the Reformation Trier remained a mainly Catholic town, but its location near the French border allowed liberalising influences. During the Napoleonic period, for example, laws preventing practicing Jews from entering public life were not enforced. One person who benefited was Baruch Marx, a talented young man who had qualified in law and aimed at a career in local administration. There were rabbis further back in the Marx family, but Baruch was an Enlightenment thinker, committed to a generalised belief in God as a support for moral ideals. Even so, his Jewish origins would have prevented advancement within the Prussian state.

After the final fall of Napoleon, the Rhineland again became part of Prussia, with some reluctance. The Rhinelanders were 'compulsory Prussians', as Frederick Engels put it (Marx and Engels 1975–2005, vol. 20, p. 224). When civil liberties for Jews were withdrawn, Baruch Marx became a Christian, like others in his position, and was christened Heinrich. Two years later, on 4 May 1818, his son Karl Heinrich Marx was born, the second of five children. Heinrich Marx had a successful career in the Court of Appeal. He tended to mix with friends who shared his liberal values, such as Johann Hugo Wyttenbach, principal of the local Gymnasium. The family lived in a comfortable part of the city. Their neighbours were the Westphalen family, rewarded for public service by ennoblement, whose daughter Jenny was to marry Karl Marx. Her more conventional older brother later became a Prussian government minister, as Marx's detractors sometimes pointed out.

Marx's social background, then, was the professional middle class. He was close to his father but not to the rest of the family, apart from one sister who later emigrated to Cape Town. Relations with his mother Henriette, daughter of a cantor in the Nijmegen synagogue in the Netherlands, were never easy. He got on better with her uncle Lion Philips, a wealthy banker who provided advances on his future inheritance. Where Marx's Trier childhood does have relevance to his later life and work is in another area: his school education.

1.2 Marx's Schooling

The young Marx attended the Trier Gymnasium. Originally a Jesuit institution, the school had been secularised but retained former Jesuit properties including extensive vineyards which supported its upkeep. Students received the education available to boys from middle-class backgrounds at the time, including a sound grounding in Greek and Latin that shows up throughout Marx's career. This humanistic model was the result of reforms introduced by Wilhelm von Humboldt, Prussian minister of education, at the beginning of the nineteenth century. Humboldt's guiding principle is expressed in the German word *Bildung*. There is no exact English equivalent, but one translation is 'self-cultivation'. The term stands for a process of growth extending across personality as a whole, as distinct from particular skills or bodies of knowledge. The ideal of *Bildung* is intended to apply both to individuals and to society, and its application to schooling is designed to bring together both of these aspects.

From the standpoint of *Bildung*, the classical curriculum is a means to an end. By providing access to the art, literature and philosophy of great past cultures, it gives students an opportunity to encounter models of achievement that will inform and guide their own aspirations. The greatest German thinkers of the period—including writers such as Goethe, Schiller and Hölderlin—tried to portray the path towards a recapturing of what they believed had been a high point in human civilisation. At the same time, the call for self-development contained a strong critical element, since it implied a rejection of many traditional claims to authority over the individual—especially those of established religion.

The principal of the Trier Gymnasium was Johann Hugo Wyttenbach (1767–1848), a friend of Marx's father and fellow member of a local club of liberal intellectuals. As a young teacher Wyttenbach had made the acquaintance of Germany's leading author, J. W. von Goethe, and discussed Kant's ideas with him. Later he became a versatile writer and editor, dealing with philosophy and history as well as education. During the Rhineland's period of liberalisation Wyttenbach brought out a book entitled *The Spirit of Religion: A Philosophical Anthology*. This collection of extracts from various thinkers presents a consistent message: genuine religion has nothing to do with dogmatic doctrines or formal practices. Rather, it consists in a freely chosen commitment to the highest values, represented in an idealised concept of God. This is the teaching of the greatest mind of the Enlightenment, Immanuel Kant. Hence, one is not surprised to find many extracts from Kant's writing, and from his various disciples and followers, although sceptics such as Hume, Gibbon and Voltaire make unexpected appearances to offer support for a purified conception of religious faith.

Kant's position on religion is that the individual's inner awareness of a moral law is the only rationally defensible basis for obedience to the will of God.

> The concept of a divine will, determined according to pure moral laws alone, allows us to think of only one religion which is purely moral, as it did of only one God. But if we admit statutory laws of such a will and make religion consist of our obedience to them, knowledge of such laws is possible not through our own reason alone but only through revelation, which, be it given publicly or to each individual in secret, would have to be a historical and not a pure rational faith in order to be propagated among men by tradition or writ (Wyttenbach 1806, p. 103).

Some of the writers included in Wyttenbach's book press a political demand for freedom of thought and belief. Religion that relies on state power is a particular target of criticism, as when Johann Heinrich Pestalozzi—better known as a pioneer of progressive education but a strong supporter of Enlightenment thought—insists that the state's only proper role is to safeguard religious tolerance within a community.

> Religion, in so far as it is genuine and true religion, is, like morality, wholly the concern of the individual person alone; its truth is not at all the business of the state, whose only responsibility is to protect and preserve the right of individuals to be true to their convictions in each case (Wyttenbach 1806, p. 85).

The Kantian conception of true religion as an individual's freely chosen commitment to the highest ideals was also the view of Heinrich Marx, as a letter written to his son at university shows: 'That you will continue to be good morally, I really do not doubt. But a great support for morality is pure faith in God. You know that I am anything but a fanatic. But this faith is a real requirement of man sooner or later' (Marx and Engels 1975–2005, vol. 1, p. 647).

At the end of his final year at school the young Marx submitted two formal essays. They are the high-minded exercises that one would expect on such occasions, but one of them, 'Thoughts of a Youth on Choosing a Vocation', contains passages that resonate with his later life. It insists on the importance of work that has genuine worth. This must be freely undertaken: 'worth can be assured only by a profession in which we are not servile tools, but in which we act independently in our own sphere' (Marx and Engels 1975–2005, vol. 1, p. 7). While no single direction is indicated, one passage points towards the study of law that the young Marx was about to begin.

> Those professions which are not so much involved in life itself as concerned with abstract truths are the most dangerous for the young man whose principles are not yet firm and whose convictions are not yet strong and unshakeable. At the same time these professions may seem to be the most exalted if they have taken deep root in our hearts and if we are capable of sacrificing our lives and all endeavours to the ideas which prevail in them (Marx and Engels 1975–2005, vol. 1, p. 8).

The principal Wyttenbach, who marked the essay, approved of the opinions expressed. He judged the essay to be 'rather good' in content but marred in places by vague and flowery language.

Marx's school experience made no great impression on him. He did not keep in touch with old schoolmates and later described Prussian education as 'only calculated to make good soldiers' (Marx and Engels 1975–2005, vol. 21, p. 399). Is this a comment on his own school experience? The Trier Gymnasium was a conventional German school of the period, oriented towards classics and the study of ancient languages. There was an alternative, proposed by reformers who wanted an approach based on the study of the nature of the child. Their preferred curriculum played down dogmatic religion and included modern languages alongside the ancient ones, as well as gymnastics. The best known of these educators was Johann Bernhard Basedow (1724–1790), founder of the *Philanthropinum*, a model school established in Dessau in 1771. Its motto was 'Everything according to nature'. In Königsberg, Immanuel Kant recommended the *Philanthropinum* to friends, reviewed Basedow in the local press and gave lectures on pedagogy using his book as a text. Although the *Philanthropinum* closed down after Basedow's death, his ideas were a lasting influence, soon to be carried further by educational reformers such as Pestalozzi.

Marx is surprisingly dismissive of this tendency, judging by a reference in *Capital* to 'the Basedows and their imitators' (Marx and Engels 1975–2005, vol. 35, p. 491). His objection is one often made by critics of progressive education: that it spends too much time on play and not enough on work. In part, this judgement simply reflects Marx's own personality. In 1857 his wife Jenny Marx described his daily routine: 'By day Karl works for his living [that is, writing articles for the *New York Herald Tribune*] and by night at the completion of his political economy' (Marx and Engels 1975–2005, vol. 40, p. 566). At times he spent the entire day making notes at the British Museum. Similarly, Marx's views about education embody a certain work ethic, or at least a recognition that while work may become freely chosen rather than imposed by class domination, it will still remain work, subject to the demands of an objective reality and often requiring effort and discipline. As he remarks in rejecting the utopian visions of Charles Fourier, 'Labour cannot become a game' (Marx and Engels 1975–2005, vol. 29, p. 97). Nor can schoolwork, in his opinion.

Marx's tastes in art and literature were the product of his education. They tended towards the classic authors of the Western canon, with some additions from the French Enlightenment, as well as English novelists dealing with the realities of a changing society: Charles Dickens and W. M. Thackeray, Charlotte Brontë and Elizabeth Gaskell (Marx and Engels 1975–2005, vol. 13, p. 664). In answering a questionnaire for his daughter Jenny's album, he named Dante, Aeschylus, Shakespeare and Goethe as his favourite poets, and Diderot, Lessing, Hegel and Balzac as favourite prose writers (Marx and Engels 1975–2005, vol. 42, p. 567). His 'aversion' was Martin Tupper, the best-selling author of a versified 'philosophy' expressing conventional Victorian sentiments. Tupper makes an appearance in *Capital* when Marx takes a swipe at various targets, starting with Jeremy Bentham, the founder of modern utilitarianism: 'Bentham is among the philosophers what Tupper is among poets. Both could only have been manufactured in England' (Marx and Engels 1975–2005, vol. 35, p. 605). In general, Marx tends to use literary sources when he is in a satirical or polemical mood. Bentham is again a case in point: 'Had I the courage of my friend, Heinrich Heine, I would call Mr Jeremy a genius of bourgeois stupidity'. This sharp edge is just one of the features of his writing that makes it quite different from the usual literature of political economy. It helps us to bear in mind that Marx is a revolutionary as well as an educator.

1.3 Doctor Marx

Marx began university studies in Bonn, not far from his home town. He made little progress and caused his father concern by engaging in typical student behaviour of that time, including running up debts and fighting a duel. After one year in Bonn, he transferred to Berlin, a university with distinguished professors and higher standards. His father had mixed feelings about the change, writing to him in the summer of 1836:

> I know that in regard to science Berlin has advantages and great attraction. But apart from the fact that greater difficulties arise there, you must surely also have some regard for your parents, whose sanguine hopes would be largely shattered by your residing so far away. Of course that must not hinder your plan of life; parental love is probably the least selfish of all. But if this plan of life could be fraternally combined with these hopes, that would be for me the highest of all life's joys, the number of which decreases so considerably with the years (Marx and Engels 1975–2005, vol. 1, pp. 677–678).

In Berlin Marx enrolled in law and attended the lectures of the legal historian Friedrich Karl von Savigny and one of the more able Hegelians, Eduard Gans. His only philosophy class was logic, taught as an introduction to Hegel's system by an orthodox disciple, Georg Andreas Gabler. A greater immediate influence was the Old Testament course of an unorthodox theology lecturer, Bruno Bauer. Nine years older than Marx, Bauer became a guiding influence, despite his departure for a position at Bonn University in 1839.

Philosophy had been important at Berlin University since its founding in 1810. Two outstanding thinkers, J. G. Fichte and Georg Wilhelm Friedrich Hegel, had occupied the chair in philosophy. Hegel's system was based in metaphysics and logic, but extended to religion and law as well. It combined rationalism with an idealism that privileged pure thought as providing a truer knowledge of reality than empirical observation or experiment. Hegel located his system within the history of philosophy as its culminating phase: his system claimed to take up all other modes of philosophy as phases in its own development. Hegel died in 1831, but his influence was renewed by the publication of his lectures on history, aesthetics, the philosophy of religion and history of philosophy. Produced from student notes, these presented his ideas more accessibly than his own books. Yet change was occurring in German thought, as it had following the Kantian revolution fifty years earlier. The completeness of Hegel's system left his orthodox disciples with little to do except edit his writings or apply his teachings to particular disciplines such as law. It was the younger 'Left Hegelians' who struck out in new directions by uncovering radical tendencies in Hegel's thought.

For the younger generation of German intellectuals during the 1840s, Ludwig Feuerbach (1804–1872) was a crucial figure. Once a student of Hegel, Feuerbach had become a powerful opponent of the Hegelian school. His departure from the University of Erlangen after challenging religious orthodoxies confirmed his status as a non-conformist. In *The Essence of Christianity* (Feuerbach 1957), the Christian idea of God is presented as an external projection of human nature. Alone among living things, Feuerbach argues, human beings are aware of their 'mode of being' or 'essential nature'—that is, of their *species*. Yet they lose touch with this reality and look for it elsewhere, in an imaginary being whose qualities are really just those of the human essence.

The rejection of conventional religion was widespread in the younger generation. More surprising was Feuerbach's critique of philosophy itself. Breaking away from the intellectualism of Hegelian idealism, he emphasises that philosophy is about human beings, their relation to nature and their feelings towards one another. All communication, he argues, arises from shared thinking, which in turn assumes a common life. Philosophy tries to separate thought from this setting, and so ends with an abstract system of concepts. Genuine knowledge, however, comes from the senses and feeling, for only these enable us to encounter actual objects. What is real is what we care about, what gives us pleasure and pain, what we love or hate. The old philosophy, Feuerbach says, treated people as just thinking beings. 'In contrast, the new philosophy joyfully and consciously recognizes the truth of sensuousness: It is a sensuous philosophy with an open heart' (Feuerbach 1972, p. 227).

Many German intellectuals embraced Feuerbach's call to engage with the world of experience and feeling. The composer Richard Wagner dramatised the redemptive power of love in his operas, and dedicated his manifesto 'The Art-Work of the Future' to Feuerbach. Another follower was the Berlin positivist Eugen Dühring, later to be a rival of Marx and Engels as a philosophical mentor for the socialist movement. Marx joined the trend but was dissatisfied by Feuerbach's reluctance to turn his commitment to human solidarity into political action. Feuerbach, he thought, was right to emphasise the natural aspect of human life, but wrong to leave out the equally important political and historical dimension, always present even in our experience of nature (Marx and Engels 1975–2005, vol. 5, p. 40). In consequence, Feuerbach's conception of activity remains disengaged from the real problems of today's human beings, oppressed by poverty and injustice. Sympathy with others is not enough, Marx concludes: a commitment to transforming the social environment is what is needed.

In Berlin Marx joined a circle of contemporaries who were radical by temperament and conviction and who, like him, had been studying Feuerbach's writings closely. He mentioned this group in a letter to his father, summarising the academic studies which, he said, had persisted during a spell of illness. 'While I was ill I got to know Hegel from beginning to end, together with most of his disciples. Through a number of meetings with friends in Stralow I came across a Doctors' Club, which includes some university lecturers and my most intimate Berlin friend, Dr. Rutenberg' (Marx and Engels 1975–2005, vol. 1, p. 19). In fact, Marx was mixing with a group that called itself by a less innocuous name: 'The Free Ones' (*Die Freien*). They met regularly at Hippel's wine bar on Friedrichstrasse, not far from Berlin University. Most were young scholars influenced by Hegel but putting his ideas to critical use, at first in theology but then in politics. A leading figure was Bruno Bauer, whom Marx hoped to follow to Bonn. The group also included his brother Edgar Bauer and several Berlin graduates now teaching at local schools. A few years later, the membership shifted. One new face was Johann Kaspar Schmidt, better known by his pseudonym, Max Stirner. Another was Frederick Engels, who combined his military service (which Marx had been excused on medical grounds) with attending lectures at the university, until his father sent him to work in the family textile business in Manchester. By then Marx had left Berlin: he met Engels only several years later and became close friends with him later still.

Marx was a student in Berlin for five years. In 1841 he decided to submit a doctoral thesis—but at the University of Jena. The reason for the shift seems to be that the Jena examination process was relatively cursory. Within a few weeks of submission, a panel of professors certified that the work 'testifies to intelligence and perspicuity as much as to erudition', and the degree of Doctor of Philosophy was awarded. Some commentators suggest that anything looking Hegelian would have been suspect in the eyes of the Berlin authorities. This is implausible: there were still prominent Hegelian professors at the university. In any case, while its philosophical vocabulary may be Hegelian, the thesis sticks to scholarship, avoiding controversial areas such as Christianity or politics.

Marx's topic is the Democritean and Epicurean philosophies of nature. There are hints of his later thought in a privileging of Epicurean materialism over the older doctrines of Democritus. In place of causal determinism, Epicurus introduces an element of spontaneity, the so-called 'swerve' of atoms that Cicero regarded as providing an escape from fatalism. Marx's account of the swerve is Hegelian, at least in its terminology. If atoms simply fell in a straight line, he asserts, they would lack 'self-sufficiency'. They would not be solid objects but just moving points. By changing direction, the atom distinguishes itself from the line and takes on an individuality that in turn determines the outcome of collisions with other atoms. It is pointless to ask for the cause of this event, Marx argues, since it is only atoms that act as causes in the materialist system, and the swerve or declination is what makes the atom an atom in the first place (Marx and Engels 1975–2005, vol. 1, p. 50).

In further discussion, Marx notes that the 'swerve' is often regarded as an arbitrary addition. Yet he considers it to be crucial to atomism: 'the law which it expresses goes through the whole Epicurean philosophy'. For example, human beings maintain their individuality by 'swerving' away from distracting influences. The gods stand apart from the world for the same reason. A further consequence is that atoms must repel one another. Here Marx notes the analogy (to which Hegel had drawn attention in his *Philosophy of Right*) between atomism and civil society, within which individuals are separate from one another.

Working notes for the thesis contain passages that some have taken as early versions of Marx's mature themes. What can happen to philosophy after its completion? Marx asks. 'It is a psychological law that the theoretical mind, once liberated in itself, turns into practical energy' (Marx and Engels 1975–2005, vol. 1, p. 85). And yet that practice (here Marx uses the word *Praxis* for the first time) is still theoretical. 'It is the critique that measures the individual existence by the essence, the particular reality against the Idea'. Having fully constructed its system, philosophy confronts this totality against the world of experience. Marx works away at the resulting contradictions in characteristically Hegelian fashion. They lead in two directions. What he calls the 'liberal' party is loyal to the philosophical system and uses it to criticise reality. In contrast is the 'positive philosophy' that adheres to reality and sees it as an indication of the deficiencies of philosophy.

By the time his doctorate was awarded, Marx had given up any idea of an academic career. He and his friends were aware that their radical ideas excluded them from university appointments. With a private income, Ludwig Feuerbach could afford to express religious scepticism, but others were less fortunate. Bruno Bauer was in no position to help, having been forced out of academic life in 1842 after attacking the Gospels as concocted fictions, a far more radical view than critical theologians such as David Friedrich Strauss. Back in Berlin, Bauer now became a journalist, as did many of the Young Hegelians—including Karl Marx.

1.4 Marx as Journalist

Marx's first paid job after leaving university was as a journalist in Cologne. The *Rheinische Zeitung* was a daily newspaper run by the socialist Moses Hess as a competitor to the conservative *Kölnische Zeitung*. Marx had already made contributions, and in October 1842 took over the editorship. Five months later the paper was closed down, but during that time Marx published several important articles of his own as well as dispatches from Frederick Engels on the condition of the working class in England. While Engels had become more radical, Marx's references to socialism were still non-committal. His main priority was a campaign against government censorship. The *Kölnische Zeitung* had argued in a leading article that the state should be seen as an educational institution, differing from schools only in having a broader scope. Marx responds that the state is certainly engaged in education, but by bringing individuals to rise above identifying themselves with particular interests and to participate in the life of the whole community. 'The leading article, on the other hand, makes the state not an association of free human beings who educate one another, but a crowd of adults who are destined to be educated from above and to pass from a "narrow" schoolroom to a "wider" one' (Marx and Engels 1975–2005, vol. 1, p. 193).

This liberal Marx is clearly a member of the Hegelian Left, with a strong belief in the concept of *Bildung*, including an integration of the individual with social institutions. The same approach is seen in an article on press censorship in a journal edited by his Berlin friend Arnold Ruge. Marx vigorously attacks the Prussian government, reviewing the history of its censorship laws over the years. He is still very Hegelian and denounces what he calls 'an unethical and materialistic view of the state'. A truly ethical state, he insists, will be a democratic one in which the members are not subordinated to central authority and may even oppose it.

Before long, Marx became disillusioned with such liberalism. He came to see the reforms needed to realise its goals as impossible within the present social system. Signs of this shift can be seen in the first examples of what was to become a recurring trait: Marx's need to distance himself from recent associates and even attack them publicly. The first target was his old mentor Bruno Bauer, now a Berlin editor engaged in social criticism that included elements of anti-Semitism. In the twentieth century Marx's essay 'On the Jewish Question' was often claimed to be itself anti-Semitic, so it is worth pausing to look at its actual content and direction.

In 1843 Bauer brought out a book entitled *Die Judenfrage* [The Jewish Question], and a shorter essay repeating its conclusions. Bauer writes as a theologian as well as social critic. He addresses the situation of Jews in a political state that is officially Christian, but his real subject is religion and 'enlightenment'. What matters most to him is not the relation of Jews to the state, but to their own religion. His view is that like Christians, they need to be emancipated from religion. Hence, Bauer refuses to support Jewish emancipation. Since ordinary

Germans are not free, he argues, Jews should not look for an emancipation of their own but simply work for the common good.

Bauer's idea of liberation owes much to Feuerbach's critique of Christianity: human beings must cease to project their own essence as an external reality that leaves them impoverished and subjected to its authority. With this in mind, Bauer asks: what would a political emancipation of Jews contribute to that end? Jews might be able to participate in public life while remaining Jews, provided that they obtain permission from the synagogue for exemptions from the Jewish law, for example, to work or carry out military service on the Sabbath. But Bauer is not satisfied with such a compromise, which he sees as a kind of hypocrisy—that is, making exceptions for one's own benefit.

This whole argument is biased by a strongly negative assessment of Judaism. Bauer assumes that given the advantages of assimilation, nobody would have a good reason to remain within the Jewish faith. He thinks that Judaism is far less developed than Christianity. At present Christianity has given rise to its own critique: where does that leave Jews? They may be pleased to see their old persecutor in trouble, but the situation reveals how backward their own religion remains. Christianity, especially in its Protestant form, has at least made the human essence its object, and so become a universal conception—whereas for Jews, loyalty is still limited to the family or the people.

> Christianity therefore stands far above Judaism, and the Christian far above the Jew, and his capacity to become free is far greater than that of the Jew, since from the standpoint that he occupies as a Christian, humanity has reached the point where a thoroughgoing revolution will heal all the damage that religion in general has caused (Bauer 1843).

Bauer concludes: 'The Enlightenment has therefore its true place in Christianity'. As the most completed religion, it is the preliminary to a liberation from religion in general. Compared to this, exemptions for Jews to engage in some business on the Sabbath are trivial. The other option open to Jews is to become Christian. But Bauer thinks it is too late for that, since Christianity has reached the end of its road. He concludes: 'If they want to become free, the Jews should not profess Christianity, but rather dissolved Christianity, dissolved religion in general: that is, enlightenment, criticism and its outcome, a free humanity' (Bauer 1843).

Bauer has redefined the 'Jewish question' as a political rather than religious issue. Marx takes a further step: he rejects Bauer's assumption that state authority is the problem. We have to apply criticism to political emancipation itself—not just to the Christian state, but to the state itself. Bauer's great mistake, according to Marx, is to confuse political emancipation with universal emancipation. In fact, we must question whether political emancipation alone can justify the abolition of Judaism and religion generally. Instead of following Bauer's assumption that the transition from Judaism to Christianity is itself a development towards emancipation, Marx now asks: what social element would be involved in an abolition of Judaism?

His answer centres upon the relation between the state and 'civil society', in which people interact as individuals, rather than as members of a family or a community. This distinction comes from the Scottish political economists, by way of Hegel's philosophy of right. Marx gives it a radical turn through his destructive criticism of the concept of the state. The two realms, he says, are like heaven and earth—but as we know, heaven is imaginary. The conflict between the individual as adherent of a particular religion and the person as a citizen is just one example of the conflict between civil society and the state. Marx's criticism of Bauer is that he fails to acknowledge the primary importance of civil society, compared to which the state is a secondary phenomenon. Political emancipation, typified by a separation of church and state, is a step forward. But religion flourishes in civil society, where everyone can follow his or her own personal whims. The United States is an example: a nation that has no official religion, but where religious denominations of all kinds gain wide support.

What we need, Bauer argues, is not freedom of religion, but freedom *from* religion—that is, the abolition of both Judaism and Christianity. Marx responds that this would only change people's behaviour on one day a week. Bauer is concerned with what the Jew does (or does not do) on the Sabbath. What about the other six days? Those are dominated by another religion—the worship of money. Here Marx uses 'Judaism' for what he supposes is the Jew's weekday occupation: making money, especially through banking and finance. As far as this goes, he comments, Jews have already emancipated themselves. In fact, taking his rhetoric a stage further, the state may be Christian, but civil society is dominated by Judaism. It is a risky metaphor, upsetting for modern ears, especially when Marx goes on to suggest that the Jewish religion corresponds closely to a civil society that revolves round money and self-interest. Yet he argues that 'it is only in the Christian world that civil society attains perfection' (Marx and Engels 1975–2005, vol. 3, p. 173). For Christianity completes the estrangement of human beings from their natural qualities and leaves them as isolated individuals. Then Judaism takes over by making self-interest the only motive for their interaction.

Marx shows no sign of taking 'the Jewish question' personally. Still, his father's legal career had depended on conversion to Christianity to satisfy the Prussian state. What if that concession had not been necessary? Bauer's rejection of Jewish assimilation could have struck Marx as an attack on Heinrich Marx. In *The Holy Family* he returns to the Jewish question, presenting his earlier response more clearly by taking direct aim at Bauer's statement that 'The Jewish question is a religious question'. No, says Marx, all religious questions must nowadays be seen as social questions (Marx and Engels 1975–2005, vol. 4, p. 108). After all, if Judaism had been overtaken as a religion and replaced by Christianity, as Bauer supposes, how can its continued existence be explained? Marx answers: 'by practical features of civil society which are fantastically reflected in that religion'. That is, Judaism survives within modern Christian society because that society's economic practice, epitomised as 'the money system', corresponds closely to the Jewish religion. Hence, if the state were consistent with its own basis in civil society, it would allow Jews every right that other citizens have, and treat their religion as a purely private matter.

The importance of these essays is that Marx moves decisively away from the critique of theology. The Left Hegelians were preoccupied with their own rejection of traditional Christianity. For Marx, atheism is just 'the last stage of theism, the negative recognition of God' (Marx and Engels 1975–2005, vol. 4, p. 110). From now on, his concern is not religion but society.

References

Bauer, B. (1843). Die Fähigkeit der heutigen Juden und Christen, frei zu werden. http://www.marxists.org/deutsch/referenz/bauer-b/1843/xx/juden.htm. Accessed 15 May 2013.

Feuerbach, L. (1957). *The essence of Christianity* (G. Eliot, Trans.). New York: Harper and Brothers.

Feuerbach, L. (1972). *The fiery brook: Selected writings of Ludwig Feuerbach* (Z. Hanfi, Ed and Trans.). Garden City: Anchor Books.

Marx, K., & Engels, F. (1975–2005). *Collected works* (Vols. 50). London: Lawrence and Wishart.

Small, R. (2005). *Marx and education*. Aldershot: Ashgate.

Wyttenbach, J. H. (1806). *Der Geist der Religion. Eine philosophische Anthologie*. Frankfurt am Main: I.C.B. Mohr.

Chapter 2
Marx's Radical Turn

Abstract Marx's early writings display the change in his direction. The 1844 *Economic-Philosophical Manuscripts* argue that private ownership of the means of production is an expression of estrangement from other human beings and from our own shared human nature. Before long, Marx is attacking philosophical materialism for its failure to engage in active struggle against class division and oppression. Yet he also rejects the individualistic solutions of the libertarian Max Stirner. Out of these debates arises the concept of 'revolutionary praxis' that informs his later political thinking. *The German Ideology* presents an approach to history that identifies the source of change within the economic 'base' of society. At the same time, Marx recognises that elements of the 'superstructure' such as education may sometimes run ahead of the economic process. Working in partnership with his friend Friedrich Engels, he writes the *Communist Manifesto*, a fiery call for the overthrow of class divisions.

Keywords Karl Marx • Max Stirner • Alienation • Historical materialism • Uneven development • Praxis

2.1 Introduction

When the *Rheinische Zeitung* was suppressed, Marx went to live in Paris. Leaving Germany was the beginning of radical changes in his outlook. The first writings to follow are known as his 'Paris' or 'Economic-Philosophical' manuscripts. They represent a change in his thinking, a further development of the new focus on social problems. Marx now sees political issues as defined not by a struggle for individual rights, but by class division and oppression. He engages in dialogue with other radical alternatives, mostly utopian, and polemicises against all forms of philosophical idealism.

The *Manuscripts* centre on the concept of *alienation*, drawn from Feuerbach's critique of Christianity but relocated in the social and political sphere. Like

R. Small, *Karl Marx*, SpringerBriefs on Key Thinkers in Education,
DOI: 10.1007/978-94-007-7657-9_2,

Feuerbach, Marx assumes a common human essence that makes possible our feelings of sympathy and love towards others. He is particularly concerned with the human capacity to interact with the external world through work—that is, an activity that engages with nature to produce an object that satisfies some human need. His target of criticism in these texts is a social system that separates us from our own productive activity and its outcomes, making these something alien and thus leaving us deprived of what should be a part of ourselves. At first sight, this looks like a consequence of private ownership of the means of production, which compels non-owners to sell their labour power in order to live. On the contrary, Marx writes: 'although private property appears to be the reason, the cause of alienated labour, it is rather its consequence' (Marx and Engels 1975–2005, vol. 3, p. 279). Because we are estranged from our own activity, we are also estranged from its products. To complete the picture, he describes what non-alienated labour would be like: it would enable us to see our products as 'so many mirrors in which we saw reflected our essential nature' (Marx and Engels 1975–2005, vol. 3, p. 228).

Often overlooked in the 1844 *Manuscripts* is a strong element of materialism, not entirely identifiable with Feuerbach's version. Labour is identified with 'the subjectivity of *objective* essential powers, whose action, therefore, must also be something *objective*. An objective being acts objectively, and he would not act objectively if the objective did not reside in the very nature of his being' (Marx and Engels 1975–2005, vol. 3, p. 336). Another theme in the *Manuscripts* that points to Marx's later thought is communism, a social system that provides an alternative to private property. His first remarks on the subject are highly philosophical. They repudiate 'crude communism', which simply turns the state or community into a kind of capitalist owner for whom everyone is a labourer. Genuine communism, in contrast, is a positive reappropriation of the human essence. Marx boldly presents this concept as the solution to a broad range of philosophical problems.

> This communism, as fully developed naturalism, equals humanism, and as fully developed humanism equals naturalism; it is the genuine resolution of the conflict between man and nature and between man and man—the true resolution of the strife between existence and essence, between objectification and self-confirmation, between freedom and necessity, between the individual and the species (Marx and Engels 1975–2005, vol. 3, p. 296).

Soon he was to take a very different view of socialism, in part through working closely with Frederick Engels, who had made a study of the English working class during his first period in Manchester and saw the issues in far more down-to-earth terms.

Marx's stay in Paris was a short one, since the Prussian government's hostility followed him around. Expelled from France at the beginning of 1845, he left with his wife and newborn daughter for Belgium. In Paris he had become closer to Moses Hess, known through the *Rheinische Zeitung*. Hess was possibly the first outright socialist Marx had met in person, even if his socialism was the philosophical kind satirised in the *Communist Manifesto* as 'true socialism'. The following three years in Brussels confirmed the course Marx would follow. He began to mix with trade unionists and working-class socialists for the first time. Just as importantly, he formed his lifelong friendship with Frederick Engels.

The two men first met when Engels visited Cologne on his way to Manchester, but did not get to know each other until spending time together in Paris in 1844. It was then that their working partnership formed. Its basis was a common outlook, but just as importantly, they formed an effective team, even if their backgrounds and personalities were different. Both were Rhinelanders, but Engels came from Elberfeld in the industrial northern region, where his father was a factory owner. His lifestyle was always a middle class one, especially in Manchester, where he mixed with the industrial bourgeoisie and even joined in their pastimes: when Marx arrived for a visit in 1864, Engels was out fox hunting (Marx and Engels 1975–2005, vol. 42, p. 63). When asked by his daughter for his motto, Marx responded with a saying often linked with Descartes: *De omnibus dubitandum*: 'Everything [is] to be doubted'. Engels' less high-minded response was 'Take it aisy [*sic*]'.

The initial period of joint work was very productive. Together they wrote two books detailing the theoretical errors of their former Berlin friends, *The Holy Family* and *The German Ideology*. Then came *The Communist Manifesto*, a work that builds on the strengths of both men, starting from an early draft by Engels alone but adding in Marx's literary flair. After that, they tended to work on individual productions, but with continual interaction. In the 1850s Marx gained a regular income by writing on current affairs for the *New York Herald Tribune*. Some articles were supplied to him by Engels, and it is hard to see much contrast except in subject matter. Engels was proud of his early military experience (the Marx family nicknamed him 'General') and covered military matters, leaving Marx to deal with politics. Both also contributed short entries on military subjects to the *New American Cyclopedia*. Engels' later commentaries on *Capital* show his clear grasp of Marx's theoretical position, good enough to give advice on its presentation. Still, it is evident that in his major work in political economy, Marx was on his own.

2.2 The Debate with Materialism

Education and the individual person are discussed in the 'Theses on Feuerbach', a short sketch of Marx's general philosophy, apparently written in 1845 although not published until much later. The title was added by Engels because most, although not all, of the 'theses' deal with Ludwig Feuerbach and develop a consistent critique of his materialism. This is signalled by the opening passage:

> The chief defect of all previous materialism (that of Feuerbach included) is that things, reality, sensuousness are conceived only in the form of the *object*, or of *contemplation*, but not as *sensuous human activity, practice*, not subjectively. Hence, in contradistinction to materialism the *active* side was set forth abstractly by idealism—which, of course, does not know real, sensuous activity as such. Feuerbach wants sensuous objects, really distinct

> from conceptual objects, but he does conceive objects, but he does not conceive human activity itself as *objective* activity (Marx and Engels 1975–2005, vol. 5, p. 3).

Marx was familiar with the materialist tradition, since his doctoral thesis had been on its earliest figures, Democritus and Epicurus. He argues that throughout its history, materialism has failed to recognise one side of human experience. It has based its claims—about the reality of the world, for example—on 'contemplation' alone. The word used is *Anschauung*, a frequent expression in German philosophy from Kant onwards but hard to translate into English: the most common rendering is 'intuition'. It refers to any experience in which something is immediately *given* to us. This covers perception and also imagination in which, as Kant puts it, we 'give ourselves' the object. An image is only in our minds, but still in some sense 'there'. We call intuitions 'empirical' when they involve *sensation*, which tells us that the object is something real. In contrast, space and time are regarded by Kant as 'pure' intuitions, ideal rather than real and yet still given, rather than constructed in our minds.

Feuerbach places great emphasis on sensory experience as well as feeling and emotion, claiming that these are what put us in touch with the outside world, including other people. Marx approves of all this, as far as it goes. But he argues that it leaves out something important: what he calls 'the *active* side'. That is not a mere oversight on Feuerbach's part, but a difference of opinion on the meaning of activity. Marx cites a passage in *The Essence of Christianity* in which Feuerbach argues that as human beings, we are in harmony with the world when we contemplate it and construct our theories in imagination.

> When, on the contrary, man places himself only on the practical standpoint and looks at the world from thence, making the practical standpoint the theoretical one also, he is in disunion with nature; he makes nature the abject vassal of his selfish interest, of his practical egoism (Feuerbach 1957, p. 113).

Feuerbach suggests that this is the attitude of Judaism, passed on to Christianity, which retains the same belief in providence and miracles—what he calls 'egoism in the form of religion'. If we judge by 'On the Jewish Question', Marx may agree. But he denies that all human activity is like this—that is, driven by selfish motives. Moreover, he argues that this prejudice gives idealism an excuse to present itself as the only philosophy that makes room for human creativity and freedom. Yet as Marx points out, the idealist is thinking of activity only as working with ideas, not with real, sensible things.

What sort of activity is missing from this debate? Marx describes it in several ways: as 'objective', 'sensuous', 'revolutionary' and 'practical–critical'. In the 1844 *Manuscripts*, objective and sensuous activity is the kind that produces material objects. This is later called 'living labour'. All living things interact with their environment and so maintain their own life processes, but human beings also maintain the forms of things outside themselves (Marx and Engels 1975–2005, vol. 28, p. 285). This purposeful behaviour is an expression of our own common nature, although under conditions of alienation we are prevented from seeing ourselves in our products. If labour were a free activity, it would be a different story.

> In my production I would have objectified my individuality, its specific character, and therefore enjoyed not only an individual manifestation of my life during the activity, but also when looking at the object I would have the individual pleasure of knowing my personality to be objective, visible to the senses and hence a power beyond all doubt (Marx and Engels 1975–2005, vol. 3, p. 227).

This is not self-interest in the narrow sense Feuerbach has in mind—in fact, it is consistent with his emphasis on shared experience. But how does it address the dilemma that Marx is concerned with here? Presumably by including a critical element: hence, the further description 'practical–critical'.

What that means emerges in the Third Thesis, which bears directly on education, provided the word is used in a wide sense, to include all of the influences that determine human development. Marx raises the question: are we just passive recipients of these influences, or do we somehow interact with them and thereby determine our own development? His reply centres on a well-known remark: 'the educator must be educated'. The whole passage is rather longer:

> The materialistic doctrine of the changing of circumstances and education forgets that circumstances are changed by men and that the educator himself must be educated. It must therefore divide society into two parts, one of which is raised above it. The coincidence of the changing of circumstances and human activity or self–changing can only be grasped and rationally understood as *revolutionary praxis*.

This is a very concentrated passage, and the implications are enormous. Marx starts out by referring to what he calls the 'materialistic doctrine' about education, and then goes on to criticise that theory. This might seem strange. Marx calls himself a materialist, and yet here we find him attacking materialism. In fact, what he is criticising is one particular version of materialism, the kind typical of the French philosophers of the eighteenth century. Let us look more closely at their ideas and Marx's response to them.

These writers proposed a radically new theory of human nature. They argued that the development of the individual person was entirely determined by social circumstances, so that all the contrasts we observe between one person and another—in personality, abilities and knowledge—are due to differences in their environments. This led them to put great emphasis upon education, where the word 'education' refers not just to formal instruction or schooling but to all the influences acting on the individual. In *The Holy Family*, Marx summarises the doctrines of the French materialist Helvétius: 'The natural equality of human intelligences, the unity of progress of reason and progress of industry, the natural goodness of man, and the omnipotence of education, are the main features in his system' (Marx and Engels 1975–2005, vol. 4, p. 130). The British social and educational reformer Robert Owen took over these doctrines, proclaiming that 'the character of man is, without a single exception, always formed for him: that it may be, and is chiefly, created by his predecessors: that they give him, or may give him, his ideas and habits, which are the powers that govern and direct his conduct' (Owen 1970, p. 140).

The materialists wanted to use education as a means of social reform. Human beings, they thought, were basically selfish. Yet with a well-designed education, people could learn that their well-being is best furthered by joining together in ensuring the general social good, rather than by seeking their separate interests. These more enlightened individuals would form a different kind of community, leading to the disappearance of most, if not all, of the evils of present social life.

Marx disagrees completely. He rejects this approach because, as he explains, it 'forgets that circumstances are changed by men and that the educator himself must be educated'. In saying this, he is making a telling objection to the materialist approach on what are really *logical* grounds. The theory talks about using education for social reform. But in making this suggestion, it is assuming the existence of some person (the 'educator') who controls the environment which in turn determines the development of newer generations. Marx thinks that the materialist theory is not entitled to make any such assumption. In fact, it is contradicting itself by doing so, because the existence of such an 'educator' is inconsistent with the deterministic premises of this standpoint. Having given society total power over individual development, one can hardly go on to talk about some individual opportunity for intervention within the social process. Hence, Marx's conclusion: that this theory divides society 'into two parts', one of which paradoxically stands above society itself.

So, what is his alternative? Marx says practically nothing about what he means by 'revolutionary praxis'. The expression is introduced to resolve the dilemma by positing a mode of activity that changes the acting person as well as the surrounding circumstances. But perhaps we can go a step further, by bringing these closer together. More specifically, each aspect is 'mediated' by the other. That is, we change ourselves by means of changing our circumstances, and vice versa. What would praxis have to be like to match this description? Marx does not explain further in the 'Theses'. Still, clues are found in his writing of the time, and especially in his dialogue with Max Stirner, as we shall see shortly.

The last of the Theses on Feuerbach is the aphorism quoted earlier: 'The philosophers have only interpreted the world in various ways; the point, however, is to change it'. Here, Marx reasserts the conclusion of his critique of the Hegelian school: philosophy cannot solve its own problems. It is likely to go on forever with the same debates unless it shifts ground and turns into social and political activity—that is, into the 'praxis' of the earlier theses.

2.3 The Debate with Max Stirner

One final look at the Berlin 'Free Ones' is in order at this point. Membership of the group changed over time. Marx went to Cologne, Bauer returned from Bonn, and Engels arrived from Elberfeld and joined the group. Another new member was

Johann Kaspar Schmidt, better known by his pen-name, Max Stirner. A decade older than Marx and Engels, he had once attended Hegel's lectures at Berlin University, but poverty and family responsibilities prevented him from completing a doctorate. While teaching in a girls' school, Stirner worked on a statement of his radically individualistic philosophy, published in 1844 as *The Ego and His Own* (Stirner 1963/1973). Marx seems never to have met Stirner, but Engels knew him well, and must have told Marx about his personality. References in their letters suggest a certain fondness for Stirner, but this did not prevent Marx from adopting the same one-sidedly negative attitude in print as he did with all their old Berlin associates.

We need to look at Stirner's philosophy of rebellion and Marx's response to it. But another reason for attention to Stirner is that he wrote on education from a teacher's standpoint. It is true that his 1834 essay 'Ueber Schulgesetze' (On school legislation) is tame stuff (Stirner 1834). It treats the school's role as defined wholly by the relation between teacher and pupil, and explains that children are to acquire religion, academic knowledge and morality through their interactions with these models of adult feeling, thinking and willing. Stirner's ideas had moved on by 1842, when he published two articles in the *Rheinische Zeitung*, on which Marx was working (and whose editor he was soon to become). In one of these, Stirner argues that the tension between art and religion, as rival approaches to the ideal, can only be resolved by philosophy. The other essay introduces the standpoint of *The Ego and His Own*. Its tone is more polemical, as the title signals: 'The false principle of our education'.

Stirner addresses a current debate over schooling. The classical ideal of an education based on ancient cultures was under challenge from those who saw the modern school as preparing learners not for university study, but for working lives in commerce and industry. These 'realists' proposed a curriculum including modern languages and practical skills, especially related to science and technology. A recent author had proposed a *Konkordat* (that is, peace treaty) between 'school' and 'life'—and, by analogy, between these rival models of schooling. Who could object to a combination of humanism with realism, one aiming at mastering the heritage of the past, the other at achieving freedom and independence within the present world? Stirner does, and goes on to accuse both sides of false beliefs about the aims of education.

What humanism and realism have in common, he argues, is that they treat knowledge as a possession—either ornamental or useful, as the case may be. That is a typical philosophical view. But what is needed, Stirner asserts, is educators who are 'more than philosophers'. We must give up thinking of knowledge as something that belongs to us and which therefore holds us back, like all possessions. 'Proper knowledge perfects itself when it stops being knowledge and becomes a simple human drive once again—the will'. Echoing Feuerbach's call for a return from abstract thought to life, Stirner states his own goal for education:

> If it is the drive of our time, after freedom of thought is won, to pursue it to that perfection through which it changes to freedom of the will in order to realise the latter as the principle of a new era, then the final goal of education can no longer be knowledge, but the will

born out of knowledge, and the spoken expression of that for which it has to strive is: the personal or free man (Stirner 1842).

Such true individuals are not produced by the school. If they exist at all, it is in spite of education. So, what is the alternative? The realists are right in wanting a practical education, but genuine practice is not getting on in life by accommodating oneself to the demands of society. The natural curiosity of children is regarded as something to be encouraged and developed, Stirner says—why not their equally natural wilfulness? He wants an education which will encourage a spirit of rebellion and creativity, a school in which the teacher is a colleague (*Mitarbeiter*). Adults must renounce their authority over children and treat them as equals. Thus, Stirner concludes, we do not need a harmony between education and life, but a complete unity of the two—a slogan that prefigures the later 'deschoolers'.

Could it be that Marx, who published this essay on education in his newspaper, was in sympathy with some of its arguments? It is noticeable that he makes no mention of it in his lengthy criticism of *The Ego and His Own* and its sequel, a reply to several reviewers, including Ludwig Feuerbach. He certainly agrees with Stirner's claim that philosophy must somehow be 'overcome' and replaced by something different. As we will see, however, from that starting point their paths diverge.

The Ego and His Own is a personal manifesto rather than a philosophical treatise. Rambling and repetitive, it is also constantly provocative and often brilliant. Stirner has one main idea: the only thing that can matter to me is myself. Everything else he has to say is a consequence of this premise. The book opens dramatically with a declaration of absolute independence. There is nothing higher than the individual that could make justified claims on him or her: no causes, no vocations, no ideals and no values. Freedom, truth, justice—all are summarily dismissed as *not my concern*. After all, Stirner argues, God and humanity are concerned only with themselves, so why should not I be the same? Freedom is not enough, since it is only negative: we can achieve it by getting rid of things. Stirner has his own word for what is really needed: 'ownness'. The presentation of this theme is structured by tracing the course of a typical human life. The child is realistic, the youth is idealistic, but the adult must be egoistic. In both cases, the third stage is not so much a synthesis of the first two as a repudiation of both in favour of the value of self-interest and 'ownness'.

Education is a recurring theme in *The Ego and His Own*. Stirner couples priests and schoolmasters as authorities who impose sweeping demands on the free individual in the name of some ideal conception of the purpose and meaning of life. Stirner attacks the progressive thinkers who advocate universal education. 'Not enough that the great mass has been trained to religion, now it is actually to have to occupy itself with "everything human." Training (*Dressur*) is growing ever more general and more comprehensive' (Stirner 1963/1973, p. 326). People are expected to 'dance to the pipe of schoolmasters and bear-leaders'. But this is simply replacing the authority of priests with other authorities.

Stirner insists again and again: there is nothing that human beings ought to do to develop themselves, no model to live up to. His positive message is one of a spontaneous exercise of natural powers. Rather than striving to attain some goal in life, we should take the lilies of the field as our model:

> The flower does not follow the calling (*Berufe*) to complete itself, but it spends all its forces to enjoy and consume the world as well as it can—it sucks in as much of the juices of the earth, as much air of the ether, as much of the sun, as it can get and lodge. The bird lives up to no calling, but it uses its forces as much as is practicable; it catches beetles and sings to its heart's delight (Stirner 1963/1973, p. 326).

He is opposed not just to Feuerbachian humanism, with its appeal to a normative essence of humanity, but also to the critical use of Hegelianism, which uses philosophical concepts to judge and condemn present realities such as the political state. Stirner however does not believe in vocations, including so-called ontological vocations: we have no obligation to realise any human essence.

There is a sharp contrast with Marx here, crucial for their philosophies of education. Stirner's shafts against socialism and communism are deftly aimed. Communism wants us all to work hard, he suggests, since it sees labour as the human 'calling'. There is some truth in this, but irony as well, given the close association between the work ethic and capitalism. According to Marx, the 'great historical mission' of capitalism is fulfilled when 'by the strict discipline of capital to which several generations have been subjected, general industriousness has been developed as the universal asset of the new generation' (Marx and Engels 1975–2005, vol. 28, p. 250). In a future society, he argues, people may well work for shorter hours, but they will feel a *need* to work which is not just for the sake of satisfying other needs. Marx believes in free activity, but understands this as work, and is scornful of what he regards as an idle notion of play, even where children are concerned. As we shall see, this attitude shows up in his proposals for school reform, especially in the content of the curriculum.

Marx's view of Stirner as a formidable challenger is evident in the hundreds of pages used to deal with him in *The German Ideology*. This is something of an intellectual show trial. Stirner has to be wrong not just on main points but in every detail, and passages where he seems to make some good point must be explained as quite wrong when read properly. At times Marx's criticism is fair enough: he knows more about Democritus and Epicurus than Stirner does, for instance. But he relies heavily on sarcasm and personal put-downs, and even labels Stirner as a 'schoolteacher': Marx does not forget who has the doctorate.

The substantial charge running through Marx's critique is that Stirner treats human life as determined by beliefs (mostly false ones about the 'human essence') and ignores the real conditions and social relations that, as Marx puts it, 'had to take the form—insofar as they were expressed in thoughts—of ideal conditions and necessary relations' (Marx and Engels 1975–2005, vol. 5, pp. 183–184). So Marx agrees with Stirner that most people's ideas about themselves and the society they live in are mistaken, but he thinks that Stirner does not see where the solution lies, and so is in the end as much a prisoner of philosophical abstraction as those he is criticising.

A crucial difference is that Stirner is profoundly anti-political. He is against political parties, since they simply replicate the authority of the state on a smaller scale by imposing conformity on their members. Accordingly, he distinguishes between revolution and 'rebellion' or 'insurrection' (*Empörung*, a word that literally means 'rising up'). Revolution means an overturning of conditions, but rebellion is driven by our discontent with ourselves and has wider change only as a further consequence. After all, Stirner reasons, if we no longer participate in the system, it will collapse of its own accord. 'Now, as my object is not the overthrow of an established order but my elevation above it, my purpose and deed are not a political or social but (as directed towards myself and my ownness alone) an egoistic purpose and deed' (Stirner 1963/1973, p. 316). The difference is explained in more detail:

> Revolution and insurrection must not be looked upon as synonymous. The former consists in an overturning of conditions, of established condition or status, the state or society, and is accordingly a *political* or *social* act; the latter has indeed for its unavoidable consequence a transformation of circumstances, yet it does not arise from it but rather from men's discontent with themselves… It is not a struggle against the established, since, if it prospers, the established collapses of itself; it is only a working forth of me out of the established. If I leave the established, it is dead and passes into decay. Now, as my object is not the overthrow of an established order but my elevation above it, my purpose and deed are not a political or social but (as directed toward myself and my ownness alone) an *egoistic* purpose and deed (Stirner 1963/1973, p. 316).

In response, Marx starts from Stirner's remark that 'a society cannot be turned into a new one as long as those of whom it consists and who constitute it remain as of old' (Marx and Engels 1975–2005, vol. 5, p. 214). Certainly they are dissatisfied with themselves, he agrees, but what does that mean?

> Dissatisfaction with oneself is either dissatisfaction with oneself within the framework of a definite condition which determines the whole personality, e.g. dissatisfaction with oneself as a worker, or it is moral dissatisfaction. In the first case, therefore, it is simultaneously and mainly dissatisfaction with the existing relations; in the second case—an ideological expression of these relations themselves, which does not at all go beyond them, but belongs wholly to them (Marx and Engels 1975–2005, vol. 5, p. 378).

Working-class revolutionaries have no intention of remaining the sorts of people they are. 'They know too well that only under changed circumstances will they cease to be "as of old," and therefore they are determined to change these circumstances at the first opportunity. In revolutionary activity the changing of oneself coincides with the changing of circumstances' (Marx and Engels 1975–2005, vol. 5, p. 214).

The last statement is almost identical with the conclusion of the Third Thesis on Feuerbach, and the surrounding text spells out the meaning of 'praxis' more clearly. Marx is emphasising a critical thinking which is also *self-critical.* However, this is not the self-criticism that leads people to blame themselves for poverty or discrimination. In the Sixth Thesis, Marx asserts that the 'human essence' is not an abstraction located within each individual person, but the totality of social relations (Marx and Engels 1975–2005, vol. 5, p. 7). Hence, he does not accept the disjunction between individual and group interests that the utilitarians take for granted. These tensions result from particular social arrangements—in particular, from private property and class divisions—and so would no longer exist as problems in a different kind of society. By arguing in this way, Marx and Engels think they can distance themselves from 'morality', or at least from the version of morality that sees social existence as a *problem* for the individual person, rather than as the necessary setting for achieving a fully human existence. If their remarks on socialism here seem utopian, it must be remembered that they also see opportunities in the here and now for anticipating the future through engaging in 'revolutionary praxis', not only as social groups but also as individuals.

2.4 The Birth of Historical Materialism

In their first joint production, *The Holy Family*, Marx and Engels distance themselves from the Young Hegelians, with Bruno Bauer as the main target. The disputes involve a degree of mockery, but are not deeply hostile. Despite Marx's polemics against Bauer, they got on well together when Bauer visited him in London ten years later. It is a pity that *The Holy Family* was published rather than *The German Ideology*, because it is the longer work that contains key pointers to what would later be labelled 'Marxism'. It begins with a firm statement of the authors' commitment to philosophical realism:

> The premises from which we begin are not arbitrary ones, not dogmas, but real premises from which abstraction can only be made in the imagination. They are the real individuals, their activity and the material conditions of their life, both those which they find already existing and those produced by their activity. These premises can thus be verified in a purely empirical way (Marx and Engels 1975–2005, vol. 5, p. 31).

The introduction goes on to outline the theory later known as 'historical materialism'. It centres on a distinction between the 'base' and 'superstructure' of society. The base is where a society maintains its existence by material production, and the way it does this is taken to determine what happens elsewhere. The model is contrasted with a rival picture which Marx and Engels clearly think is very common: that what happens in society is determined by ideas and concepts. Later Marx summed up his theory in this way:

> In the social production of their existence, men inevitably enter into definite relations, which are independent of their will, namely relations of production appropriate to a given stage in the development of their material forces of production. The totality of these relations of production constitutes the economic structure of society, the real foundation, on which arises a legal and political superstructure and to which correspond definite forms of social consciousness. The mode of production of material life conditions the general process of social, political and intellectual life. It is not the consciousness of men that determines their existence, but their social existence that determines their consciousness (Marx and Engels 1975–2005, vol. 29, p. 263).

Some important points need to be noted here. First of all, the 'base' contains two elements: the forces of production (that is, the tools and machines that produce the things people need in everyday life) and the relations of production (that is, the circumstances that determine who owns and controls these things). In contrast, the social superstructure is quite diverse: it includes law, science, religion and philosophy. Now comes a crucial claim: that forces and relations of production can match one another or come into conflict.

> At a certain stage of development, the material productive forces of society come into conflict with the existing relations of production or—this merely expresses the same thing in legal terms—with the property relations within the framework of which they have operated hitherto. From forms of development of the productive forces these relations turn into their fetters. Then begins an era of social revolution. The changes in the economic foundation lead sooner or later to the transformation of the whole immense superstructure (Marx and Engels 1975–2005, vol. 29, p. 263).

When such conflict becomes insoluble within the existing social structure (Marx and Engels call this a 'contradiction'), the outcome is social revolution. They claim to have several examples from past history, but the most important is evidently the rise of capitalism, which is closely tied to changes in material production from handicrafts to manufacture and then to the large-scale use of machinery.

It was not long before Marx came to see that a simple economic explanation would seldom work for political and social changes over a shorter term. In his analysis of Louis Bonaparte's 1851 seizure of power in France, he offers a more subtle account of state power, suggesting that in certain circumstances the state apparatus may seem to achieve an independence that allows it to be controlled by some group or even a single individual without any evident class identity. Yet he goes on to argue that this status is only apparent: 'the state power is not suspended in mid air' (Marx and Engels 1975–2005, vol. 11, p. 186). In this case, Louis Bonaparte was able to challenge the power of the middle class because he had the support of other classes—above all, the rural peasantry—and on that basis could claim (speciously, on Marx's view) to represent the French people as a whole.

The need for caution in applying the base/superstructure model is emphasised again in Marx's 1857–1858 drafts for *Capital*, which introduce the theme of 'unequal' (or 'uneven') development.

> The unequal development of material production and e.g. art. In general, the concept of progress is not be taken in the usual abstract form. With regard to art, etc., this disproportion is not so important and not so difficult to grasp as within practical social relations themselves, e.g. in culture. Relation of the United States to Europe. However, the really difficult point to be discussed here is how the relations of production as legal relations enter into uneven development. For example, the relation of Roman civil law (this applies in smaller measure to criminal and public law) to modern production (Marx and Engels 1975–2005, vol. 28, p. 46).

What is meant by 'culture' here? The German word is *Bildung*, and so another translation could be 'education', especially given the contrast with culture in the usual sense: 'art, etc'. That reading also makes better sense of what follows: 'Relation of the United States to Europe'. We know from elsewhere that Marx considered public education in the United States to be more advanced than education in Britain, France and Germany, even though the American economic system was at that time not as advanced as those countries (Small 2005, pp. 146–147).

So it provides a good illustration of his point: the development of the cultural 'superstructure' may run ahead of its economic base—or, for all we know, lag behind it. This is not too surprising where artistic, philosophical and religious life is concerned. We do not expect these to develop in close parallel with material production, because they are not what Marx is calling 'practical social' activities. In sharp contrast is law. Here he wonders how any modern nation can still have a legal system based on ancient Roman law (which Marx had to study as a university student, one might recall). Given these two extreme cases, we can see that education lies somewhere in between. That is the basis on which Marx is able to advance proposals for school reform. He can acknowledge the limits to what can be achieved within a capitalist society, yet still look for opportunities for an education that runs ahead of the present state of things. In Chap. 4, we will see how he does this in more detail.

2.5 The Communist Manifesto

In 1847 Marx and Engels joined a small group of exiled German radicals which was about to change its name from 'League of the Just' to the more militant 'Communist League'. They were invited to prepare a general statement of its objectives. The two men seized the opportunity to put their own stamp on the party's official philosophy and objectives. Printed in February 1848, their text became a classic statement of political philosophy.

The *Manifesto of the Communist Party* makes a sharp break from its 'League of the Just' background by taking a hard-headed approach to politics. Gone is any suggestion of a secret society avoiding public attention. Rather, the *Manifesto* declares that 'the Communists disdain to conceal their aims'. Missing too are rebellious poses, utopian visions and idealistic slogans such as 'All men are brothers'. Instead, Marx and Engels set out to ground their assertions and proposals in the reality of social change.

> The theoretical conclusions of the Communists are in no way based on ideas or principles that have been invented, or discovered by this or that would-be universal reformer. They merely express, in general terms, actual relations springing from an existing class struggle, from a historical movement going on under our very eyes (Marx and Engels 1975–2005, vol. 6, p. 498).

The *Manifesto* opens with a bold statement of its most basic premise: 'The history of all hitherto existing society is the history of class struggles'. Different societies have contained different kinds of classes, defined in terms of their economic position. What follows in the first section is a survey of the historical developments that have led to modern society. It is the story of one class's rise to supreme economic and political power: the 'industrial middle class'.

Anyone reading just the opening pages of the *Manifesto* might see it as a celebration of capitalism. The bourgeoisie, we are told, has brought about revolutionary changes in every area of society. 'It has accomplished wonders far surpassing

Egyptian pyramids, Roman aqueducts, and Gothic cathedrals'. It has brought about new and improved means of communication and transport, creating a world market and thus a world community. And most of all, it has greatly increased human productivity and created great wealth. But how has it achieved this? Part of the answer involves radical changes in both the means and relations of production. As Adam Smith had explained, labour becomes simplified with the use of machinery and an advanced division of labour. People no longer work for themselves, but as members of a society in which everyone depends on everyone else. The worker is no longer tied to a particular occupation, but is expected to learn new kinds of labour as technology gives rise to new industries.

Yet none of these changes are specific to a capitalist system. Marx always separates means of production such as machinery from the social relations that determine their use in a particular society—that is, who owns them and gets the benefit and who exercises power over their use. 'Machinery is no more an economic category than the ox who draws the plough. The present *use* of machinery is one of the relations of our present economic system, but the way in which machinery is exploited is quite distinct from the machinery itself' (Marx and Engels 1975–2005, vol. 38, p. 99). The crucial point is this: whereas the worker uses tools, machinery uses the worker in this context. Here we see the intersection between form of production and social relations of production at its most intense. Marx is committed to saying that only in a capitalist system does the machine become the subject and the worker the means.

Above all, the *Manifesto* emphasises that capitalism is a revolutionary force. It promotes constant innovation and expansion in society's forces of production. The effects of this imperative extend throughout every level of society. Capitalism undermines all the older beliefs, customs and values:

> The bourgeoisie cannot exist without constantly revolutionising the instruments of production, and thereby the relations of production, and with them the whole relations of society. Conservation of the old modes of production in unaltered form, was, on the contrary, the first condition of existence for all earlier industrial classes. Constant revolutionising of production, uninterrupted disturbance of all social conditions, everlasting uncertainty and agitation distinguish the bourgeois epoch from all earlier ones. All fixed, fast-frozen relations, with their train of ancient and venerable prejudices and opinions, are swept away, all new-formed ones become antiquated before they can ossify. All that is solid melts into air, all that is holy is profaned, and man is at last compelled to face with sober senses, his real conditions of life, and his relations with his kind (Marx and Engels 1975–2005, vol. 6, p. 487).

Picking up the themes of Marx's 1844 *Manuscripts*, the *Manifesto* asserts that capitalism has reduced all social relations to the simple economic relation of buying and selling. Such passages have a startling ambiguity. Do the authors approve of all this cultural destruction? At one moment they mock the old conventions as delusions that humanity is well rid of, using expressions like 'philistine sentimentalism', and in the next they condemn their replacement by economic relations best expressed in the impersonal language of money. What that brings about is, in fact, a new superstition, in its own way more insidious than the old ones. It is what Marx later calls the 'fetishism of commodities'.

One of the achievements of capitalism that Marx values most is its tendency to disregard national boundaries. 'The bourgeoisie, by the rapid improvement of all instruments of production, by the immensely facilitated means of communication, draws all, even the most barbarian, nations into civilization'. This has implications for culture as well as commerce.

> In place of the old wants, satisfied by the productions of the country, we find new wants, requiring for their satisfaction the products of distant lands and climes. In place of the old local and national seclusion and self-sufficiency we have intercourse in every direction, universal interdependence of nations. And as in material, so also in intellectual production. The intellectual creations of individual nations become common property. National one-sidedness and narrow-mindedness become more and more impossible, and from the numerous national and local literatures, there arises a world literature (Marx and Engels 1975–2005, vol. 6, p. 488).

After a dozen pages celebrating the achievements of the bourgeoisie, Marx and Engels change their tone, and a darker side of the picture emerges. These developments are admirable by themselves, yet in the social conditions of capitalism their benefits are distributed very unfairly. In fact, such accomplishments act against the interests of the working class by reinforcing the power of the bourgeoisie, although they could be used in a very different way, to promote the general good.

But is that likely to happen? What could bring about such a revolution? As Marx likes to put it, the middle class is like the sorcerer's apprentice who cannot control the powers he has summoned up. The capitalist system is liable to economic cycles that alternate between periods of rapid expansion and sharp downturns leading to periods of stagnation or recession. As these economic swings become greater, short-term solutions no longer work. The great problem that capitalism's ruling class now faces is just the one identified in Marx's base/superstructure model: a mismatch between the social relations of production and the forces of production that they are supposed to manage. To explain the consequences of this crisis, a new historical actor is now introduced into the story: the working class.

This class has been brought into being by capitalism, which needs a large supply of workers, especially in the cities where large-scale industry is located. Even here Marx and Engels find something to praise: the bourgeoisie 'has created enormous cities, has greatly increased the urban population as compared with the rural, and has thus rescued a considerable part of the population from the idiocy of rural life' (Marx and Engels 1975–2005, vol. 6, p. 488). Now attention turns to the condition of the working class, in order to show why it is crucial to the fate of capitalism in crisis. The *Manifesto* describes the progressively sharper division of society into two directly opposed classes: those who own the means of production and those who own nothing but their ability to labour, which they are forced to sell in order to go on living. So the argument of the first section comes to a dramatic conclusion, by identifying the latest version of the class conflicts that have characterised all past societies. Other social classes have been absorbed into the working class, or simply faded away. They are no longer actors in the historical drama. 'Of all the classes that stand face to face with the bourgeoisie today, the proletariat alone is a really revolutionary class'. The revolution that the proletariat alone is capable of will have a unique character: the outcome must be a classless society, since there are no remaining options for the rule of one class over others.

The next section introduces the communist movement and claims it to be the only political force capable of speaking and acting on behalf of the working class as a whole. The central principle of communism is 'abolition of private property'. That needs explanation, because what is meant is not personal possessions but *capital*—that is, property that is used to maintain the economic power of one class over another. If anything, Marx says elsewhere, capitalism is hostile to the first kind of property, because it needs a class that owns nothing but its own ability to labour. Here another typical Marxian theme is introduced: in bourgeois society, capital is a power in its own right, which controls living human beings.

The *Manifesto* goes on to rebut other objections to communism: that it abolishes morality and religion, the family and patriotism. Its response is a vigorous counterattack: all these have already been destroyed by capitalism and replaced by market forces. The section concludes by listing a set of ten demands that it says will be carried out in the first phase of a social revolution. They include various exercises of state power, designed to eliminate the free hand that capitalism has managed to acquire. One of these demands is: 'Free education for all children in public schools. Abolition of children's factory labour in its present form. Combination of education with industrial production, &c., &c.' (Marx and Engels 1975–2005, vol. 6, p. 505).

The third and fourth sections of the *Communist Manifesto* are less important for today's readers. They contain polemics against other factions of the period, few of later interest. For example, the 'true socialists' (none is named, but the titles cited point to Moses Hess) are accused of dressing up French socialism with German philosophical terminology. Allies in Paris, Marx and Hess had fallen out over leadership issues when Marx moved to Brussels, and remained at odds from then on (although twenty years later, Hess was supportive of Marx's *Capital*). Readers might not realise that the ridicule directed against phrases such as 'alienation of the human essence' is just as applicable to Marx's own writing of the Paris period—or, for that matter, to his dialectical treatment of value in the 1859 *Contribution*, toned down in the first volume of *Capital*, and further still in its second edition.

After all this, the *Manifesto* ends by returning to its main theme with a ringing call to revolution: 'The proletarians have nothing to lose but their chains. They have a world to win'.

References

Feuerbach, L. (1957). *The essence of Christianity* (G. Eliot, Trans.). New York: Harper and Brothers.

Marx, K., & Engels, F. (1975–2005). *Collected works*, 50 vols. London: Lawrence and Wishart.

Owen, R. (1970). V. A. C. Gatrell (Ed.), *A new view of society*. Harmondsworth: Penguin Books.

Small, R. (2005). *Marx and education*. Aldershot: Ashgate.

Stirner, M. (1834). Ueber Schulgesetze. http://gutenberg.spiegel.de/buch/4219/14. Accessed 19 May 2013.
Stirner, M. (1842). *The false principle of our education, or, Humanism and realism* (R. H. Beebe, Trans.). http://tmh.floonet.net/articles/falseprinciple.html. Accessed 14 May 2013.
Stirner, M. (1963/1973). *The ego and his own* (S. T. Byington, Trans.). New York: Libertarian Book Club. 1963; reprint ed., New York: Dover Books.

Chapter 3
Capitalism and Education

Abstract Marx's major work is *Capital*. In it, he sets out to uncover the working of the capitalist mode of production, starting with the simplest economic categories but showing that their true meaning is realised only within the fully developed capitalist system. Marx poses a question: how can profit be made from employing wage labour? His eventual solution depends on positing a continual interaction between the market circulation of commodities and the very different process of production: metaphorically speaking, between society's surface and its interior. Only by seeing the total picture can one grasp the reality of class domination and the ability of one class to possess the products of another's labour. At the same time, Marx depicts the historical process through which this social revolution occurred and, drawing on the reports of British factory inspectors, describes the effects of the Factory Acts which included a provision of schooling for children employed in factory labour.

Keywords Karl Marx • Education • Capitalism • Exchange value • Factory acts • Factory schools

3.1 Introduction

The *Communist Manifesto* made little public impact, although French and English editions soon appeared. Before long, the Communist League had undergone internal divisions and moved to Cologne. There its leaders were prosecuted and imprisoned for 'attempted high treason', and the League was dissolved. A new version of the *Rheinische Zeitung* was revived under the sponsorship of an unstable mixture of liberals and communists. 'The editorial constitution was simply the dictatorship of Marx', Engels later wrote. Marx's first essays in political economy appeared as articles. Other contributions came from Engels and their friend Wilhelm Wolff (to whose memory the first volume of *Capital* was eventually dedicated). The paper

R. Small, *Karl Marx*, SpringerBriefs on Key Thinkers in Education,
DOI: 10.1007/978-94-007-7657-9_3, © The Author(s) 2014

began in June 1848 and the circulation had risen to 6,000 by its suppression in May 1849, according to Engels (Marx and Engels 1975–2005, vol. 26, p. 128). The main editorial policy was the establishment of a united democratic republic in Germany. This meant opposing, on the one hand, those who wanted a single nation but a monarchy and, on the other, the liberals who wanted a federation of autonomous republican states, following the Swiss model. The paper campaigned strongly for a war against conservative and expansionist Russia, to bring about the restoration of Poland but also to help in the unification of Germany.

The year 1848 saw an outbreak of political turmoil in many European countries. When the *Neue Rheinische Zeitung* was closed down by alarmed local authorities, Marx went to Paris, while Engels, always drawn to military life, joined a volunteer corps in the Palatinate, led by August Willich, a member of the Communist League. After that rising failed, he avoided arrest by escaping to Switzerland and made his way back to England.

In August 1849 Marx arrived in London, where he was to live until his death in 1883. For a while, much of his time went on the factionalism of the German refugee community. He was increasingly impatient with rival voices within the socialist movement, and especially with uneducated ones, liable to be swayed by advocates of 'labour money' or workers' co-operatives. His main source of income came from writing articles for the *New York Herald Tribune*, edited by Charles Dana. As a working journalist, Marx was a versatile commentator on current affairs, ranging from British and French politics to international conflicts such as the Crimean war and the Indian insurgency of the 1850s. The writing tasks were shared with Engels, reluctantly employed in the Manchester office of the textile business partly owned by his father. But Marx formed the intention of making a major contribution to political economy, a scheme that occupied him for the following thirty years.

From here on, Marx is primarily a political economist or, rather, a critic of political economy. The discipline carrying this name had emerged a hundred years earlier, primarily owing to Adam Smith (1723–1790), the Glasgow professor of moral philosophy whose book *The Wealth of Nations* made the case for the free market and its 'hidden hand'. For Marx, political economy was the intellectual counterpart of capitalism, and its development closely reflected the bourgeoisie's rise to social and political domination. Smith and his greatest successor David Ricardo were the theorists Marx most respected, because they presented capitalism as a revolutionary force. In contrast, later economists set out to defend and rationalise what was now an established social order. The closer he comes to his contemporaries, the more Marx makes use of his extensive vocabulary of contempt.

Marx's analysis of modern society, centring on the relations of production that enable one class to grow in wealth and power at the expense of others, was a huge task to which he devoted the rest of his working life. During the first part of this period, he was still in cramped lodgings in Soho, not far from the British Museum. The best description we have of his life there comes from a Prussian spy who visited him at home in 1853. This anonymous individual reported to his masters:

> When you go into Marx's room, smoke and tobacco fumes make your eyes water to such an extent that for the first moment you seem to be groping about in a cavern, until you get used to it and manage to pick out certain objects in the haze. Everything is dirty and covered with dust, and sitting down is quite a dangerous business. Here is a chair with only three legs, then another, which happens to be whole, on which the children are playing at cooking. That is the one that is offered to the visitor, but the children's cooking is not removed, and if you sit down, you risk a pair of trousers. But all these things do not in the least embarrass Marx or his wife. You are received in the most friendly way and cordially offered pipes, tobacco and whatever else there may happen to be. Eventually a clever and interesting conversation arises which makes amends for all the domestic deficiencies, so that you find the discomfort bearable. You actually get used to the company, and find it interesting and original (McLellan 1981, pp. 35–36).

In undertaking a definitive account of the capitalist mode of production, Marx had committed the rest of his working life. He managed to bring out only two instalments, and the first is something of a trial run. Published in 1859 under the title *A Contribution to the Critique of Political Economy*, it corresponds to the first sections of *Capital*, dealing with commodities and money. Despite the promise of the heading 'Capital in General', readers do not get to capital and its mode of production. The Preface to this draft contains a review of Marx's past work and a preview of his overall programme which make valuable reading. The chapters themselves are hard going, overloaded with dialectical apparatus, and it is hard to see just where they are leading without hindsight gained from knowledge of *Capital*.

Marx had intended to write a series of further instalments, but eventually decided to start again. The task kept on expanding. After a further decade of work he had a vast collection of notes and drafts of chapters on all aspects of a capitalist economy. The manuscripts known as *Grundrisse* later attracted attention for their inclusion of some philosophical themes that are less visible in *Capital*: for example, they throw a useful light on the notion of 'living labour'. But it was not for another eight years that the first volume of *Capital* finally appeared.

In February 1867 Marx wrote to Engels recommending a story by one of his favourite authors, Honoré de Balzac. 'The Unknown Masterpiece' (Balzac 1831) is about Frenhofer, a great artist who has spent twenty years working on one painting, only to discover that the picture has been so overworked that there is no longer a visible image, only a confused mass of lines and colours. Marx describes this grim story as a masterpiece, 'full of the most delightful irony' (Marx and Engels 1975–2005, vol. 42, p. 348). There is certainly irony here, given the plot's parallel with his own prolonged struggle to write *Capital*. Submission dates had come and gone for years, but a manuscript was now ready for his publisher in Hamburg, overdue but at least finished. Marx no doubt felt that he had escaped Frenhofer's fate. Still, he died sixteen years later with masses of material still waiting to be put into shape. The first volume takes us as far as the completed establishment of the capitalist system and its re-establishment in distant parts of the world. The grand plan would have followed the course of capitalism from its high point through to an unprecedented crisis caused by a sharp decline in the rate of profit, and foretelling its downfall.

Even so, the completed first volume of *Capital* can be called a masterpiece. Unlike the painting in Balzac's story, the picture has not disappeared under a mass of detail. The most common complaint of readers is over the difficulty of the first chapters, a ready excuse for giving up on the work. On the advice of his friend Engels, Marx toned down his dialectical presentation of the commodity form and the emergence of money, relegating the details to a separate Appendix. He changed his mind in preparing the second edition—the first had actually sold quite well—and brought them back into the opening chapter. Hence, anyone approaching *Capital* is faced with the task of coming to terms with its most challenging aspects early on.

3.2 Value, Commodities and Money

The book's opening passage is recycled from the 1859 *Contribution*, which began: 'The wealth of bourgeois society, at first sight, presents itself as an immense accumulation of commodities, its unit being a single commodity' (Marx and Engels 1975–2005, vol. 29, p. 269). So, we are concerned with the capitalist system from the start. As the *Manifesto* pointed out, capitalism has produced far more wealth than all previous modes of production. Yet, what is wealth? Is it a great quantity of consumable goods? Within a capitalist society that would, in fact, be an unusual and bad situation: 'The accumulation of commodities in great masses is the result either of overproduction or of a stoppage of circulation' (Marx and Engels 1975–2005, vol. 35, p. 584). The single commodity, Marx goes on to explain, has two aspects, and consumability or usefulness is only one of them. As will become clear, it is another kind of value that constitutes wealth in the sense that matters to capitalism.

As well as what Marx calls 'use value', that is, the ability to satisfy some human need, commodities have what he calls *exchange value*, or simply *value*. They would not have this unless they are useful in some way, but it is not the same thing as usefulness. If I produce something in order to sell or exchange it rather than to consume it myself, then it has no use value *for me*. Rather it is a commodity from the start, and the first task of *Capital* is to explain what this means.

Value is a strangely abstract concept, common to objects that are completely different in all their 'sensuous' qualities. What can they have in common that explains it? Marx now sets out his labour theory of value: the price of any commodity is determined by the labour time necessary to produce it. By itself, this idea is not original. David Ricardo had stated it, although he had not gone on, as Marx does, to explain how profit is made under capitalism. Since that applies to labour power as much as to any other commodity, it serves as a theory of wages, which are just the price of labour power. Education comes in here in so far as training is needed for certain kinds of labour. The less training is needed for a job, the lower will be the wages of the worker.

Marx is well aware that actual prices fluctuate according to supply and demand. But this does not explain the level around which the variation occurs: that is still determined by the commodity's real value, so that exchange value and market price coincide when supply and demand balance each other (Marx and Engels

1975–2005, vol. 20, p. 118). However, to say that an object's value is measured by the amount of labour time that goes into producing it misleading, since what is meant is not actual time—that would make the products of lazy or inefficient workers worth more—but the time that is 'socially necessary'. The concept of value goes hand in hand with a generalised conception of human labour. This can exist only in a society where commodity exchange has become the universal mode of interaction and, further, where a dispossessed working class is able to live only by selling its capacity to supply this labour to produce commodities. Marx concludes that 'Labour time as the measure of wealth posits wealth itself as based on poverty' (Marx and Engels 1975–2005, vol. 29, p. 94). In a different kind of society, wealth would be measured not by labour time but by free or 'disposable time', available for the development of individual personality.

The theoretical strategy here is quite complex. The simplest concepts are introduced first, yet they gain their full meaning only from the eventual outcome. That is, the concepts of exchange value and the abstract human labour that determines this kind of value are fully realised only within the developed capitalist mode of production. In this system they are present not just in thought but in daily life. As Marx puts it, 'This reduction appears to be an abstraction, but it is an abstraction which is made every day in the social process of production' (Marx and Engels 1975–2005, vol. 29, p. 272). For the worker in a capitalist system, labour is experienced as something already generalised. It does not matter what kind of work one does, since to the employer, labour is just a means for producing surplus value. It does not matter to the worker either. 'The fact that the particular kind of labour is irrelevant corresponds to a form of society in which individuals easily pass from one kind of labour to another, the particular kind of labour being accidental to them and therefore indifferent' (Marx and Engels 1975–2005, vol. 28, p. 41). Marx adds that the best place to find this general adaptability is the United States, a point which will be repeated in his argument in support of 'polytechnical' education in *Capital.*

At one level, the account is about commodities and their exchange, then about the invention of money, and then about money as profit-making capital. This is what the political economists tell us. For Marx, there is another story altogether, one that is less apparent and yet offers a far better understanding of social reality. This inside story is all about *value* and about its counterpart within human life: abstract generalised labour. Capitalism is where value takes over and drives the entire economic process. That is its historical importance. Marx makes a pointed aside: 'Objects that in themselves are no commodities, such as conscience, honour, &c., are capable of being offered for sale by their holders, and of thus acquiring, through their price, the form of commodities' (Marx and Engels 1975–2005, vol. 35, p. 112).

But how did this dominance come about? The story of value begins with commodity exchange. It appears first as exchange value, seen when very different things are regarded as equivalent for the purpose of transferring ownership. Then comes a transformation: 'the exchange value of the commodity assumes an independent existence in money' (Marx and Engels 1975–2005, vol. 32, pp. 317–18). Unlike other commodities, money is not removed from circulation to be used or consumed, but stays there to act as an embodiment of value. All this is taken a step further when money turns into *capital*:

> It is not only an independent expression of value as in money, but dynamic value, value which maintains itself in a process in which use values pass through the most varied forms. Thus in capital the independent existence of value is raised to a higher power than in money (Marx and Engels 1975–2005, vol. 32, p. 318).

It is true that exchange value exists in bartering goods or in buying and selling them using money. But there value is not the 'subject' that makes everything happen. Material production is carried out in order to satisfy human needs and wants for things to use or consume. What matters most about the products of labour is their 'use value', determined by the various properties and qualities that enable them to satisfy human demands. When needs arise again, there is new production and exchange of commodities. This is not what drives production in a capitalist society. There, production is just a means for capital to increase itself through profit. But how this happens remains to be seen.

Marx's account of the commodity as a form of value concludes with a section on 'the fetishism of commodities', which opens in dramatic style: 'A commodity appears, at first sight, a very trivial thing, and easily understood. Its analysis shows that it is, in reality, a very queer thing, abounding in metaphysical subtleties and theological niceties' (Marx and Engels 1975–2005, vol. 35, p. 81). As an object that satisfies human needs and is the product of human labour, it is not mysterious. But these properties alone do not make it a commodity. When it is exchanged a further property comes to light, one that is distinct from the qualities we see or feel. This is its *value*. Corresponding to value is an equally abstract property of the labour that went into producing the commodity. As well as being some particular activity, it is also abstract human labour. That in turn expresses the social relations between those who exchange commodities. In any society that has a division of labour, each individual's labour has a social character, since the products are passed on to others for their use. If they are made in order to be exchanged, the labour itself acquires this new aspect, over and above its natural qualities.

This outcome is a false impression, Marx explains. Because our attention is on the object itself, we suppose that its value—what determines its exchangeability with other products—is just a property of the object, although not one that can be seen or felt.

> A commodity is therefore a mysterious thing, simply because in it the social character of men's labour appears to them as an objective character stamped upon the products of that labour; because the relation of the producers to the sum total of their own labour is presented to them as a social relation, existing not between themselves, but between the products of their labour (Marx and Engels 1975–2005, vol. 35, pp. 82–83).

In other words, things seem to take on a life of their own. He calls this 'fetishism', by analogy with the religious projection of human qualities into the external world. Primitive religions attribute human qualities to animals and plants, inanimate objects and forces of nature. In this case it is the value of commodities, a property quite separate from their physical form, that is the spiritual element. Here Marx adapts the analysis of Christianity offered by Feuerbach and his followers. When we speak of God we are really speaking of human beings, but at the same time admitting that human beings have failed to realise their own possibilities. So it is with the commodity.

Such fetishism, Marx suggests, occurs only in a society that runs by the production of commodities. Ancient society was not like this, except for trading between nations. In mediaeval society, the serf worked either for himself or for his feudal lord—but in the second case, his labour involved a personal relation, not a relation between things. In a capitalist social system, commodities seem to enter into relations with one another and to develop personalities of their own, or rather the same personality in every case. Marx tells us that the commodity is 'a born leveller and a cynic' and 'in love with money' (Marx and Engels 1975–2005, vol. 35, pp. 93, 117). Similarly, money is the universal go-between, a seducer and debaser of human values. Later capital will figure as a powerful and ruthless being for whom human beings, including the owners of capital, are merely pawns in its relentless pursuit of increase.

3.3 Inside the Black Box of Capitalism

In *Capital*, the explanation of the employer's ability to make a profit proceeds in what Marx likes to call a 'popular' manner. He starts by posing a puzzle that the capitalist needs to solve: how can a profit be made through buying and selling commodities?

Buying cheap and selling dear is not the answer. The socialist writer John Bray had supposed that the worker is simply cheated by being paid less than what the employer receives from him is worth (Marx and Engels 1975–2005, vol. 6, pp. 139–42). Marx disagrees. After all, such behaviour is much the same as robbery, and that does not create wealth, but simply redistributes the wealth that already exists (Marx and Engels 1975–2005, vol. 35, p. 173). What is more, while simply raising a commodity's price may occur, it cannot be the general practice for an economic system. Since every participant is a buyer as well as seller, whatever is gained in one role will be lost in the other. Hence, the only outcome will be price inflation, with no advantage to anyone.

The worker, Marx explains, seems to be selling his labour to the capitalist. In reality what he sells is his *labour power*—that is, the ability to work in a particular way for a particular time. Having bought that commodity, the capitalist uses it by having the workers work for the agreed time. The wages of the worker correspond to the value of his labour power: they are not, Marx insists, his share in the price of the commodity that he produces for the capitalist. After all, that is never his property. Thus, the capitalist's profit is made by using his money to buy labour power which, in the process of production, gives rise to products that are worth more than those that went into the process. He buys a commodity which has the unique property of turning itself into another commodity with greater value.

In sharp contrast to this means-end reasoning is the corresponding transition from money to capital in the 1857–1858 *Grundrisse*. There Marx puts on a display of conceptual legerdemain that certainly does look like an *a priori* construction, even if he takes care to remind us that the corresponding process in the real world can occur only when modern means of production have become available. His intention is to show that value by its own nature undergoes development. First, the two sides of the commodity, exchange value and use value, turn into a distinction between money and other commodities. Then the drive for full realisation—a very Hegelian assumption—produces a higher version: the contrast between capital and labour. Labour in its abstract, general form is the essence of value. Capital too is value, which increases itself by passing back into the element of living labour, giving up its independent existence to become a process again (Marx and Engels 1975–2005, vol. 28, p. 194). Only now are use value and exchange value completely interdependent, each mediating itself through the other. Thus, dialectical reason has produced the basic mechanism of the capitalist mode of production.

Marx's account of profit made from labour leads to an important discussion of the difference between social appearance and reality. It opens up the gap between the apparent working of society, as experienced by those who take part on a daily basis, and the real process. In everyday life we see transactions between buyers and sellers, which include the exchange of wage labour for wages. Like all market interactions, this is assumed to be a voluntary agreement between equals. Hence, Marx writes: 'In the totality of existing bourgeois society, this postulation as price and its circulation, etc., appears as the superficial process, below which, in the depths, quite other processes occur in which the apparent equality and freedom of individuals disappear' (Marx and Engels 1975–2005, vol. 28, p. 179).

Even if we make this distinction, does it help us to understand the unfairness of the system? What happens on the surface of society is fair, since it is an equal exchange of commodities, assuming that market competition enables them to be bought and sold at their actual values. What happens in the interior (that is, in the realm of production, where labour is realised) is also fair—according to a different standard. Purchasers of a commodity are normally entitled to use or consume it as they please, whatever others may think. In the capitalist workplace, equality no longer applies (Marx and Engels 1975–2005, vol. 35, p. 186). The employer has the right to determine the work done by the wage labourer and to claim the products as his own (Marx and Engels 1975–2005, vol. 35, p. 195). Since labour produces more than its upkeep requires, the capitalist makes a profit from the purchase and consumption of labour power. Marx comments: 'this circumstance is, without doubt, a piece of good luck for the buyer, but by no means an injury to the seller' (Marx and Engels 1975–2005, vol. 35, p. 204).

Readers may be taken aback. Does Marx really believe that there is no injustice in the way an employer makes a profit from the labour of others? Here as elsewhere, his critique of political economy has a strongly ironic tone. Taken by itself, this interaction is fair by the standards of the exchange and consumption of commodities. So, where is the injustice? It is seen only when both are taken together, and the process through which value increases itself is taken as a totality. When we look at that bigger picture, everything changes. Having established his basic account of capital and wage labour, Marx shifts towards a different perspective. The key here is that production is seen as a continuous cycle. Marx calls this 'reproduction'. He says that it 'gives a new character to the process, or rather, causes the disappearance of some apparent characteristics which it possessed as an isolated discontinuous process' (Marx and Engels 1975–2005, vol. 35, p. 567). One of these is just the appearance of fair exchange.

> The relation of exchange subsisting between capitalist and labourer becomes a mere semblance appertaining to the process of circulation, a mere form, foreign to the real nature of the transaction, and only mystifying it (Marx and Engels 1975–2005, vol. 35, p. 582).

His claim is when we get to this level, a description of reality will use the language not of exchange, but of appropriation. The latter is semblance. That is, it is located in the relation of observers in particular positions to the reality, and is determined by the nature and, in particular, the limitations of their standpoint. Here Marx uses two rather different contrasts: between semblance and reality, and between the surface of an object and its inner content. A surface is not an illusion, of course. It is as real as an interior; but what happens on the surface cannot be explained in its own terms alone. The hiddenness of the inside can be understood literally, since Marx is talking about what goes on behind the doors of the capitalist factory or workshop. There the notion of an agreement between independent and equal individuals is set aside in favour of a relation of one-sided power. The employer is in full control.

Still, we cannot simply say that the appropriation of surplus value is something that goes on in secrecy. Surplus value may be produced within a workplace, but it is not realised as profit until products are sold in the public world of circulation. Those profits are then used to buy labour power, and so we return to the 'depths'. We cannot ignore the surface, then, because what is important is the continual movement between surface and interior. Profit becomes capital, so that the process is repeated and becomes a continuous cycle, driven by its own dynamic rather than needing any outside motive power. A single exchange is a one-off event, arising outside the economic process and leading outside again, but here 'circulation itself returns back into the activity which posits or produces exchange values'. That is, it leads back to production, from which in turn arises new circulation. Only when money becomes capital can circulation return to its origin in this way, closing the circle and making the conceptual structure a dynamic one, as Marx assumes that it must be to capture the reality that it represents.

When the relation between employer and employee is seen as having a starting point and end point, it is simply assumed that the employer has money to invest as capital. How this comes to be the case is another story. Marx is scornful of the apologists who suggest that the capitalist owes his starting position to thrift and self-discipline. A better answer is a privatisation of public assets, whether common land or (as is more likely today) state-owned investments. When we shift to the ongoing process, this 'primary accumulation' is left behind. In the long run, capital comes from profit previously made from production involving wage labour. Now the process has turned into a closed circle—or rather, a spiral of increasing production. Some of the profit will be consumed by the employer, and some will go on rent or interest. There remains profit that will become capital. In fact, capital is now effectively composed of past profits. Hence, Marx says, we can see the worker's wages as a share of the product, even though within any particular transaction, the product and its sale come later (Marx and Engels 1975–2005, vol. 35, p. 567).

This is even clearer if we consider, instead of individual capitalist and worker, the two classes who, it must be remembered, are supposed to make up society as a whole. There is no free agreement here. Bernard Shaw thought that the workers in Marx's account were paralleled by Richard Wagner's Nibelungen, forced into slavery by the ring-wielding dwarf Alberich.

> The very wealth they create with their labour becomes an additional force to impoverish them; for as fast as they make it it slips from their hand into the hands of their master, and makes him mightier than ever. You can see the process for yourself in every civilised country today, where millions of people toil in want and disease to heap up more wealth for our Alberics (Shaw 1902, p. 10).

Sometimes Marx explains the process of profit making in terms of a division of the working day into two parts. Borrowing from earlier socialist writers, he calls these 'necessary' and 'surplus labour' (Marx and Engels 1975–2005, vol. 32, p. 374) and then, by extension, also calls them 'paid labour' and 'unpaid labour', although he concedes that these are loose expressions, since what is bought by the employer is strictly not labour but labour power (Marx and Engels 1975–2005, vol. 35, p. 534).

This enables him to draw a comparison with previous social systems based on class domination. With slavery all labour is unpaid labour, of course, since there is no agreement to any kind of exchange. Still, some of it is necessary labour in the sense that it goes to replace the cost of maintaining the slave's existence, so the rest could be called surplus labour. In the Middle Ages, serfs were allowed to work for themselves provided that, at certain times, they also worked without payment for their feudal lord (Marx and Engels 1975–2005, vol. 20, pp. 132–133). But, Marx says, what is the difference between the serf who works three days on his own land and three days on his lord's estate, and the factory worker who spends six hours a day in necessary labour and another six hours in surplus labour—that is, half of his working day in paid labour and half in unpaid labour? The only difference is that the two kinds of work are evident in the first case but hidden in the second. They cannot be pointed to because both are present in every period of work time, however small. Further, wages are paid by agreement for the whole working week. Hence, this inner division is completely hidden, and so therefore is the element of forcible appropriation.

Once again, we have to distinguish appearance from reality. Marx observes: 'As, owing to the form of wages, the whole of labour appears to be paid for, the unpaid part of it seems necessarily to come not from labour but from capital, and not from the variable part of capital but from the total capital' (Marx and Engels

1975–2005, vol. 43, p. 21). Hence, the usual notion of profit 'is only an illusory manifestation of surplus value'. These conclusions illustrate an important point. *Capital* is hard to follow just because capitalism is hard to understand. All class societies involve the power of one class over others, but in the past this has usually been maintained by an open use of force. It is doubtful whether slaves in ancient societies accepted their position in the scheme of things as natural and right, despite St Paul's advice to obey their masters. Capitalism, in contrast, is consistent with a liberal democracy in which people have the right to speak freely and even vote for opponents of capitalism. That does not mean that it can be taken at face value.

3.4 Marx as a Social Historian

Volume One of *Capital* builds up to a powerful climax with the historical emergence of capitalism, made possible by the expropriation of what now becomes the working class from any ownership of the means of production (such as land, tools and, later, machinery). Marx concludes that capitalism is based on the abolition of individual property. But, he writes, capitalist production gives rise to its own negation 'with the inexorability of a law of nature'. This is not a return to the old model of private property, but rather a new kind of property, based on co-operation and common access to the means of production—a first description of a future classless society.

Along the way, there are three long sections dealing with historical developments in Britain. The availability of material, including many official reports, was one reason for this inclusion. These passages are the result of Marx's days of research in the British Museum. Most of the material was added in the 1860s and so also has the advantage of being up to date. But there is a more important reason. The processes that Marx is describing had begun earlier and gone further in England than in any other country. In France, a large part of the population were still rural peasantry—an important factor in French society, as Marx makes clear in his analysis of political events there, *The Eighteenth Brumaire of Louis Bonaparte*. Germany had a large industrial working class, but not a modern state in which the bourgeoisie could exercise full control. And the United States was still about to undergo its main period of industrialisation. So England was Marx's obvious choice as the paradigm case for describing the emergence of the capitalist mode of production.

These are the parts of *Capital* that Marx recommended to a friend as 'the most immediately readable' for someone who might be put off by the abstractions of the early chapters (Marx and Engels 1975–2005, vol. 42, p. 490). They were not part of the original plan but added during the final few years of work, thanks to Marx's painful attacks of carbuncles, which, he explained, prevented him from concentrating on theoretical arguments (Marx and Engels 1975–2005, vol. 42, p. 224). In effect, he reclaims the ground of Engels' *Condition of the Working Class in*

England, using similar sources but bringing the descriptions up to date. Whatever Marx's reasons for adding this material, it contributes a welcome balance to the work, bringing out the human meaning of what would otherwise be a relatively abstract analysis. Now the passion and moral force that have been driving the theoretical account are allowed to emerge and express themselves in passages whose intensity ensures that their message will stay in readers' minds.

The first of these historical sections is entitled 'The Working Day'. It follows on the analysis of surplus value which shows how the profit made by the employer is proportional to the amount of labour power he is able to convert into actual labour. Marx has already shown that surplus value is not made in any particular part of the working day, as argued by Nassau Senior in his 'last hour' theory, according to which employers' profit would be eliminated by a reduction of work from twelve to eleven hours. The length of the working day is not fixed, even by the worker's apparent agreement to work for a whole day in exchange for his wages. The capitalist naturally wants to make this day as long as is practicable, while the worker wants to keep it down to a 'normal' length. So, how is the outcome decided? Marx says: 'Between equal rights force decides' (Marx and Engels 1975–2005, vol. 35, p. 243). The two social classes are engaged in a continual struggle over the length of the working day. Marx draws extensively on the reports of factory inspectors such as Leonard Horner to show how systematically British employers abuse their power over workers by forcing them to work round the clock. His illustrations include horrific stories, but such events are an inevitable consequence of the situation he has described in the vocabulary of economics. Now his language becomes vivid and angry: 'But in its blind unrestrainable passion, its were-wolf hunger for surplus labour, capital oversteps not only the moral, but even the merely physical maximum bounds of the working day' (Marx and Engels 1975–2005, vol. 35, p. 271).

In the second half of this chapter, Marx discusses British political debates over working hours. Legislation to shorten the working day is only a reversal of the lengthening that occurred in earlier centuries, going back to the fourteenth century. Marx comments that the punitive twelve hours of work required by the old workhouses are the normal expectation of their modern counterpart, the factories of capitalist industry. The re-establishment of a 'normal' working day from 1833 onwards has involved a long political campaign, marked by legislation often not backed up by means of enforcement and resisted by employers, as Leonard Horner's testimony makes clear. But the British working class is taking the lead and setting an example for other countries to follow. Marx concludes by citing the resolution adopted by the International Working Men's Association (and prepared by himself): 'the limitation of the working day is a preliminary condition without which all further attempts at improvement and emancipation must prove abortive' Marx and Engels 1975–2005, vol. 35, 305–306).

The second historical section comes not long afterwards, following a section dealing not with the length of the working day, but the proportion of the necessary labour and surplus labour that it contains. Clearly, the capitalist must aim at increasing what Marx calls 'relative surplus value'. But how? By making labour more productive. What follows is an account of the changes in material production associated with the transition to the capitalist system. Marx starts with a consideration of the division of labour that picks up where Adam Smith left off. He emphasises the rise of machinery and its effects on the nature of labour. Parallel to this history of technology, which he planned to explore further in a later volume of *Capital*, is a political drama involving struggles over the working day, the use of child labour, and the combination of schooling and work for young people.

The third historical discussion in *Capital* is about the origins of capital in so-called 'original accumulation'. At the same time, it is a history of the formation of the British working class and the elimination of the older rural classes from which it was drawn. The ending of serfdom had created a nation of free peasant proprietors in England. However, the enclosure of common land and the suppression of the monasteries transferred ownership of the means of production into new hands. It enabled one class to gain a monopoly of wealth and power. The authority of the state was used to issue 'decrees by which the great landowners grant themselves the people's land as private property, decrees of expropriation of the people' (Marx and Engels 1975–2005, vol. 35, p. 715). Driven off the land by laws penalising vagrancy, whole populations were turned into a homeless workforce at the disposal of employers of wage labour. Those who stayed became landless day-labourers. Marx emphasises that this original accumulation of capital was brought about by outright expropriation, using the forms of law to cover up a campaign of violence and injustice.

In these narrative sections we get the history of capitalism told in vivid detail. In the theoretical parts of the book, Marx is restrained in spelling out the human meaning of the processes he is describing, in order to get across the conceptual development. His historical account makes up for that by describing the brutality and human suffering committed by the new class bent on gaining domination over an entire nation.

Having reached this point, Marx adds a final chapter on the 'theory of colonialism'. This looks like an appendix or side track from the main themes, although of special interest to readers from 'colonial' countries. Marx's point is that we can see the history of capitalism being retraced in these laboratories. The British colonists in Western Australia, he writes, came with supplies to establish their settlement but forgot to bring one thing with them: the social relations of England. On arrival, they were taken aback to find themselves with no servants to make their beds and bring water from the river (Marx and Engels 1975–2005, vol. 35, p. 753). The leading British promoter of colonial schemes, Edward Gibbon Wakefield, had a solution. Colonists would be prevented from becoming independent settlers by using government policy to set a high price on land—a comment on the real relation between capitalism and state power. This, Marx says, shows that Wakefield had discovered 'the truth as to the conditions of capitalist production in the mother country' (Marx and Engels 1975–2005, vol. 35, pp. 752–753). Capitalism owes its origin to a revolution in which one social class uses state power to gain ownership of the means of production. It was not long before the colonial societies had acquired many of the main features of the industrial system—a successful replication of the earlier social experiment.

3.5 Schooling and the Factory Acts

Education appears in *Capital* within a discussion of the working day and child labour. Large-scale industry inevitably leads to special factory legislation. First of all, the Factory Acts made a minimal provision for sanitary conditions and safety precautions in the workplace. It is a striking comment on capitalism, Marx observes, that these forcible reforms should be necessary. It also refutes the myth that, in a competitive society, the common welfare is furthered by each promoting his own personal advantage. But then, even Adam Smith had conceded a need for public education, if only, as Marx puts it, 'prudently, and in homoeopathic doses' (Marx and Engels 1975–2005, vol. 35, p. 368). What Smith had not anticipated was the demand for child labour in factories which eventually led to special measures to ensure that child workers would not be altogether deprived of a basic schooling.

In an 1859 article about British industry published in the *New York Herald Tribune*, Marx wrote:

> The half-time system founded upon the principle that child labour should not be permitted unless, concurrently with such employment, the child attend some school daily, is objected to by the manufacturers on two grounds. They object to their responsibility of enforcing the school attendance of the half-times (children under 13 years of age), and they find it cheaper and less troublesome to employ one set of children instead of two sets, working alternately 6 hours. The first result, therefore, of the introduction of the half-time system was the nominal diminution to nearly one half of the children under 13 years employed in factories (Marx and Engels 1975–2005, vol. 16, p. 207).

One important influence on Marx's thinking about schools and working children, and the source of much of the information used in *Capital*, was the British reformer Leonard Horner (1785–1864). Marx had a high opinion of Horner, and paid tribute to his memory in *Capital*.

> Leonard Horner was one of the Factory Inquiry Commissioners in 1833, and Inspector, or rather Censor of Factories until 1859. He rendered undying service to the English working class. He carried on a life-long contest, not only with the embittered manufacturers but also with the Cabinet, to whom the number of votes given by the masters in the Lower House, was a matter of far greater importance than the number of hours worked by the 'hands' in the mills (Marx and Engels 1975–2005, vol. 35, p. 234).

Horner belonged to a family prominent in Scottish intellectual life and was linked with its English counterparts: his daughter Mary married the geologist Charles Lyell, through whom he came to know Charles Darwin. Horner studied chemistry and geology at the University of Edinburgh and then went into his father's linen business. He was active in promoting education in Edinburgh, helping to set up the School of Arts, which provided classes in scientific subjects for trades, and the

Edinburgh Academy, an alternative to the established High School. By the time Horner became a factory inspector, he already had a successful career in both business and science behind him.

In 1838 Horner published an English translation of the French writer Victor Cousin's report on education in Holland. His lengthy introduction drew out conclusions for Great Britain. It described the existing state of factory schools set up in consequence of the Factory Acts, and made criticisms that would become familiar in later years: there were too few schools, the teachers were unqualified, and the children were taught to read but not to understand what they read.

> It must be abundantly clear by this time, that the maxim, *laissez nous faire*, however true in matters of trade, is applicable only to a limited extent in education, and least of all in the case of such schools as we are now considering (Cousin 1838, p. xvi).

Countries such as Holland and Prussia had introduced public education with good results, disproving the fears raised by 'alarmists' that such measures would undermine the stability of society by 'sowing the seeds of discontent and revolution' (Cousin 1838, p. xvii).

In 1833 Horner had been appointed as one of the four inspectors authorised under the Factory Act to monitor and report on observance of the regulations governing child labour. For three years he was in charge of the inspectors for Scotland and Northern Ireland, before being transferred to the north of England, the centre of British industry. From 1836 to 1860 he was Chief Factory Inspector in Lancashire. Horner threw himself into the task. He sent his deputies into factories (although they were not allowed into the main production areas) to check on the owners' observance of the Factory Act rules about ages of children and school attendance. He also went himself. It was hard to tell the real ages of children, he wrote to his wife in 1837. The best way is to go by their teeth: 'I am becoming rather knowing in that way for I have looked into so many little mouths lately' (Lyell 1890, p. 352).

Horner's writings provide an account of the human side of industrialisation. In a letter accompanying his 1838 report on the Manchester area, he writes: 'scarcely a week passes in which my superintendents and I do not find ourselves cramped, and often frustrated, in our endeavours to obtain the full advantages and protection which it was the intention of the legislature to secure to children and young persons by this law'. Yet Horner was not an opponent of child labour. In fact, he opposed a proposal to reduce the working week of children between 12 and 13 years to 48 hours. Further, he did not always blame the factory owners, but drew attention to the complicity of parents in the employment of their underage children.

> In a visit to a mill near Bury on the 23rd of November last, I noticed a girl who was working, as I was informed, twelve hours a day, and had been doing so for more than two years, who appeared to me very young to have a certificate of thirteen; and on examining her father, by whom she was employed as his piecer, he admitted that she was between eleven and twelve years of age. On calling for her certificate I found that it was dated the 17th of August 1836. Here, then, was a father, in the receipt of good wages and in regular employment, who had been knowingly working his own child 12 hours a day, and that too

> from the time when she was little more than nine years old. It is not at all improbable that he was one of those who sent up petitions calling on Parliament to interfere for the protection of the poor factory children, 'the white slaves,' who were so cruelly over-worked by 'the hard-hearted, avaricious masters.' On showing the certificate to the surgeon, whose signature it bore, he could give me no explanation of it, on account of the distance of time; but from his respectability, I have no doubt that it must have been fraudulently obtained (Horner 1839, p. 15).

The factory school system was not popular with employers, and many looked for ways to avoid the burden that it imposed on them. They found the need to organise working shifts allowing children to attend school inconvenient. Some simply dismissed the children between the ages of 9 and 12, for whom schooling was required.

Even before reading these reports, Marx was familiar with Frederick Engels' account of British schooling in his 1845 book *The Condition of the Working Class in England*. Engels draws on the evidence of the Children's Employment Commission to show that legislation to make school attendance compulsory for child workers had been ineffective.

> The means of education in England are restricted out of all proportion to the population. The few day schools at the command of the working-class are available only for the smallest minority, and are bad besides. The teachers, worn-out workers, and other unsuitable persons who only turn to teaching in order to live, are usually without the indispensable elementary knowledge, without the moral discipline so necessary for the teacher, and relieved of all public supervision (Marx and Engels 1975–2005, vol. 4, p. 407).

Engels notes that school attendance laws had been opposed by the manufacturers. 'It cannot be otherwise: the bourgeoisie has little to hope, and much to fear, from the education of the working class'. Nevertheless, he concludes optimistically, even without schooling the working class could grasp the injustice of its social position. 'The English working man who can scarcely read and still less write, nevertheless knows very well where his own interest and that of the nation lies. He knows, too, what the especial interest of the bourgeoisie is, and what he has to expect from the bourgeoisie'.

Marx gives credit to the education clauses of the British Factory Acts for containing progressive elements. One of these is perhaps surprising to the modern reader: the combination of education with manual labour. Marx accepts the claim that children learn more when only part of the day is devoted to schooling.

> Paltry as the education clauses of the Acts appear on the whole, yet they proclaim elementary education to be an indispensable condition to the employment of children. The success of those clauses proved for the first time the possibility of combining education and gymnastics with manual labour, and, consequently, of combining manual labour with education and gymnastics. The factory inspectors soon found out by questioning the schoolmasters, that the factory children, although receiving only one half the education of the regular day scholars, yet learn quite as much and often more (Marx and Engels 1975–2005, vol. 35, pp. 485–486).

He quotes Robert Baker, one of the chief factory inspectors, who wrote in his October 1865 report: 'The system on which they work, half manual labour and half school, renders each employment a rest and a relief to the other; consequently, both are far more congenial to the child, than would be the case were he kept constantly at one'. Baker goes further, claiming that children attending school on a half-time basis 'make nearly as much actual progress' as children attending full time—that is, they learn more in relation to the time spent in school (he does not say not more overall, as Marx suggests). Baker was not wholly disinterested, since he claimed to be the inventor of the 'half-time system' (Lee 1964, p. 86). Still, on the strength of his testimony, Marx arrives at a conclusion that amounts to a political policy on child labour and schooling:

> From the Factory System budded, as Robert Owen has shown, the germ of the education of the future, an education that will, in the case of every child over a certain age, combine productive labour with instruction and gymnastics, not only as one of the methods of adding to the efficiency of production, but as the only method of producing fully developed human beings (Marx and Engels 1975–2005, vol. 35, p. 486).

In the next chapter, we will see how Marx tried to gain acceptance for this policy and to make it a full-scale programme for educational reform.

References

Balzac, H. de (1831). The unknown masterpiece (M. Neff, Trans.). http://www.gutenberg.org/files/23060/23060-h/23060-h.htm. Accessed 1 June 2013.

Cousin, V. (1838). *On the state of education in Holland, as regards schools for the working classes and the poor* (L. Horner, Trans.). London: John Murray.

Horner, L. (1839). Report of Leonard Horner, Esq., Inspector of Factories, for the Quarter ending the 31st of December 1838. Reports of the Inspectors of Factories to Her Majesty's Principal Secretary of State for the Home Department, for the Half-Year ending 31st December 1838 (pp. 15–18). London: W. Clowes and Sons.

Lee, W.R. (1964). Robert Baker: the first doctor in the factory department. Part one. 1803–1858. *British Journal of Industrial Medicine, 21*(2), 85–93.

Lyell, K.N. (Ed.). (1890). *Memoir of Leonard Horner, F. R. S., F. G. S. Consisting of letters to his family and from some of his friends (Vol. 1)*. London: Women's Printing Society.

Marx, K., & Engels, F. (1975–2005). *Collected works* (Vol. 50). London: Lawrence and Wishart.

McLellan, D. (Ed.). (1981). *Karl Marx: Interviews and recollections*. Totowa: Barnes & Noble Books.

Shaw, G.B. (1902). *The perfect Wagnerite: A commentary on the Nibling's ring* (2nd ed.). London: Constable.

Chapter 4
The Politics of Schooling

Abstract With the first volume of *Capital* completed, Marx returns to political activity in the 1860s. As a leading member of the International Working Men's Association, he prepares the education policy adopted at its 1866 congress. Marx's plan for the public school combines mental and physical instruction with a polytechnical training designed to promote the all-round work skills needed not only for full personal development but also for coping with a changing world of production. At later meetings of the IWMA General Council we see Marx in political debate, defending his education policies and spelling them out in greater detail. A major problem area for him is the role of the state in education. Aware of the danger of political indoctrination, Marx wants the state to fund and support public education, but without becoming 'the educator of the people'. With that in mind, he recommends a localised school system that follows the North American model.

Keywords Karl Marx • Public schools • Mental education • Vocational education • Polytechnical training • State

4.1 Introduction

When the Marx family moved from Soho to Hampstead in 1856, it was with three children: Laura and Jenny, 11 and 12 years old, and the infant Eleanor. Three other children had been born and died during this most trying of periods for the family. The older girls had received some tutoring in Soho. Their music teacher was Wilhelm Pieper, another German radical in exile. He played some of Richard Wagner's 'music of the future' for Marx, who remarked that it 'makes one afraid of the "future", including its poetical music' (Marx and Engels 1975–2005, vol. 40, p. 8).

R. Small, *Karl Marx*, SpringerBriefs on Key Thinkers in Education,
DOI: 10.1007/978-94-007-7657-9_4, © The Author(s) 2014

The American Civil War was a blow to the family in cutting off the income that Marx received from writing for American publishers. However, his financial situation improved with two substantial inheritances in 1863 and 1864: £600 from his mother and £800 from his old friend Wilhelm Wolff, for many years a teacher in Manchester. He gratefully dedicated the first volume of *Capital* to Wolff's memory. Even so, Hampstead was a move upward in social terms compared with Soho, and living costs were higher, especially when the Marxes moved to a more expensive rented house in the same neighbourhood. Despite the cash windfalls, new money troubles began to occur. During one bad spell, Marx wrote to Engels, justifying his decision to relocate the family home:

> It is true that the house is beyond my means, and we have, moreover, lived better this year than was the case before. But it is the only way for the children to establish themselves socially with a view to securing their future, quite apart from everything they have suffered and for which they have at least been compensated for a brief while. I believe you yourself will be of the opinion that, even from a merely commercial point of view, to run a purely proletarian household would not be appropriate in the circumstances, although that would be quite all right, if my wife and I were by ourselves or if the girls were boys (Marx and Engels 1975–2005, vol. 42, p. 172).

The two oldest girls were enrolled at the South Hampstead College for Ladies. This private school was run by two teachers in nearby Haverstock Hill Road, almost next to the present location of a modern comprehensive school. The girls did well in their studies. In 1858 Marx wrote proudly to Engels that 'little Jenny has received the first general prize in the first class (which also includes the English prize) and little Laura the second. They are the youngest in the class. Jenny also got the prize for French' (Marx and Engels 1975–2005, vol. 40, p. 337). But the expenses—not only school fees but extra charges for art, languages and music, which apparently would not have been needed for boys—turn up just as often in letters. 'The girls are growing up very quickly and their education, too, is becoming expensive', Marx wrote. 'At the ladies seminary they frequent, they are having private lessons with an Italian, a Frenchman and a drawing master. Now I have also got to find a chap for music' (Marx and Engels 1975–2005, vol. 40, p. 127).

Apart from these optional subjects, what sort of education was provided by the South Hampstead College for Ladies? A clue comes from the page written in 1865 by the ten-year-old schoolgirl Eleanor Marx, in her sister Jenny's 'Confessions' album, which contains candid contributions from the Marx daughters' social circle (including the family dog Whisky, who names the naturalist Buffon as his favourite author). As 'the vice you detest most' Eleanor nominates 'Eves's Examiner', and as 'the vice you excuse most', 'Playing the truant' (Omura et al. 2005, pp. 244–245). Most school pupils of the time would have understood. *The School Examiner* (Eves and Eves 1852) was a small book written by two school teachers, Charles and Georgiana Eves, for use as a classroom text by British pupils. Eleanor Marx would have been dealing with the 'Examiner' every day at the College for Ladies, and so we can form a good picture of the school's curriculum, as well as its pedagogy—and even make some guesses as to the reasons for her detestation.

The *Examiner* contains 100 pages of quizzes, each containing about 40 questions. Most are simply tests of memory. They are organised under headings: Bible History ('What was the fate of Zeeb?', 'Of whom was Judas Iscariot the son?', 'Why was the Almighty displeased with David for numbering the people?'), Geography ('Name the chief rivers of England', 'In what part of the world was the first habitation of man?', 'Where is New Zealand?'); English History ('What was the dress of the ancient Britons?', 'Name the wives of Henry VIII'); English grammar ('What is a noun?'; 'When should the subjunctive be used?'); and Roman history ('Why did Tullia throw a footstool at her charioteer?', 'Who was Virginia?', 'What happened to Rome in Nero's reign?'). The arithmetic tests tend to be exercises in calculation, often involving converting quantities between inches, pounds and quarts, and the lesser known units used in particular trades, such as ells, nails, pipes, butts and poles. A few of the *Examiner*'s questions seem open-ended ('What are the manners of the Afghans?'), but for these too there is a correct answer, provided for teachers in a companion publication, *Key to the School Examiner*. There we learn that the Afghans 'are simple in their manners, and very hospitable' (Eves and Eves 1854, p. 21).

The pedagogy implied by *Eves's Examiner* is not hard to guess, since its opening pages give teachers instructions on how to use the book. Children should submit written answers to the teacher, and after being corrected these should be carefully entered, together with the questions, in an exercise book, enabling the pupil's handwriting to be assessed. The authors state that when this procedure is followed 'the subject of the exercise will be found to be indelibly impressed on the memory'.

None of this would have suited Eleanor Marx particularly well. Of the three Marx children surviving to adulthood, she was most like her father in personality—energetic and independent, with a strongly rebellious spirit. But despite the family's money problems, its mode of life included a relatively conventional schooling for the children. For Marx, his personal situation was one thing and the condition of the working class another, needing to be carefully considered in making recommendations about their educational needs.

4.2 The Debate Over Factory Schools

With the first volume of *Capital* finally near completion, Marx returned to political activism in the 1860s. By then things had changed, and the battle lines were more clearly defined. Marx was aware of current trends and kept them in mind when suggesting reforms that might occur before any general transformation of society. He drew extensively on British sources of information in proposing guidelines for schooling, which became the official policy of the International Working Men's Association, later known as the 'First International'. The practical political side of Marx's approach to education belongs to his involvement in this international socialist movement in the 1860s and 1870s. Its first congress, held in Geneva in

1866, passed a resolution on education which was drawn up by Marx and set out his practical programme; and in later discussion he defended and extended the ideas in the programme. If our aim is to find out what Marx wanted schools to be like, this is where to look.

The IWMA policy is consistent with the *Communist Manifesto*'s call for free public education, combined with 'industrial production', but goes into more detail, especially in relation to the school curriculum. Headed 'Juvenile and Children's Labour (Both Sexes)', it begins with an endorsement of the part-time approach to children's schooling.

> We consider the tendency of modern industry to make children and juvenile persons of both sexes co-operate in the great work of social production, as a progressive, sound and legitimate tendency, although under capital it was distorted into an abomination. In a rational state of society *every child whatever*, from the age of 9 years, ought to become a productive labourer in the same way that no able-bodied adult person ought to be exempted from the general law of nature, viz.: to work in order to be able to eat, and work not only with the brain but with the hands too (Marx and Engels 1975–2005, vol. 20, p. 188).

This is a strong statement, and in *Capital* Marx defends a similar standpoint. He quotes supporting evidence from factory inspectors' reports and adds a footnote on an earlier British writer on education. 'John Bellers, a very phenomenon in the history of political economy, saw most clearly at the end of the 17th century, the necessity for abolishing the present system of education and division of labour, which beget hypertrophy and atrophy at the two opposite extremities of society' (Marx and Engels 1975–2005, vol. 35, p. 491). After quoting Bellers' remarks on the value of labour for children and the harmful effects of 'idle learning', Marx adds a comment of his own: 'A warning, this, by presentiment, against the Basedows and their modern imitators'.

John Bellers (1654–1725) was a Quaker merchant and social reformer who in 1695 published a proposal for a 'College of Industry'. Marx's source of information is Robert Owen, who reprinted Bellers' pamphlet and drew attention to the similarities between its educational proposals and his own, although it also resembles the 'home colony' movement of the late nineteenth century. Bellers considers that a combination of work and education for children is better than keeping them in the schoolroom for a full day:

> Four hours in a morning, and four in an afternoon, is too long to tie a child to his book; it's hard for a man to be tied upon one subject so long, much more is it toilsome to children, whose natures are weak, and love change; it hurts their spirits, makes them out of love with their books, and loseth much time; the children might be employed to more profit; a labouring man will hold longer at work, than a thinking man in his study: Men will grow strong with working, but not with thinking: Who have stronger bodies than labourers, and weaker bodies than great students? Labour adds oil to the lamp of life when thinking inflames it (Bellers 1695, p. 16, with spelling modernised).

Marx quotes the last sentence with approval. He seems to agree with the whole passage, taking it to support his endorsement of the factory school system of his own time.

Marx was also impressed by Nassau W. Senior's address on education to the 1863 Social Sciences Congress in Edinburgh, quoting it as well in this passage. This is a surprising turnabout, given the background. As the first professor of political economy at Oxford University, Senior followed the teachings of Thomas Robert Malthus and Adam Smith closely. He figures in *Capital* as the butt of some of Marx's more sardonic criticisms—for example, of his having '"discovered", in opposition to Ricardo's determination of value by labour, that profit is derived from the labour of the capitalist, and interest from his asceticism, in other words, from his "abstinence"' (Marx and Engels 1975–2005, vol. 35, p. 238). Marx spends several pages in ridiculing this term:

> It has never occurred to the vulgar economist to make the simple reflexion, that every human action may be viewed as "abstinence" from its opposite. Eating is abstinence from fasting, walking, abstinence from standing still, working, abstinence from idling, idling, abstinence from working, &c. (Marx and Engels 1975–2005, vol. 35, p. 592).

Senior had disputed with Leonard Horner over working hours and factory schooling. He protested against government interference in the running of factories, using arguments that are still familiar. The people most harmed by restrictions on employment will be the workers themselves, he urges. How can they learn a trade if they are not allowed to work until the age of thirteen? Moreover, if legal regulation is too demanding, manufacturers will simply move their businesses to other countries.

Marx followed this dispute with interest and indignation at Senior's argument against the reduction in the working day on the grounds that the profit made by the employer depended on the so-called last hour (Senior 1844). But he evidently felt that Senior had learned a lot over the following years, and suggested that this showed how modern industry was capable not only of revolutionising production but 'of also revolutionising people's minds' (Marx and Engels 1975–2005, vol. 35, p. 486). Senior's 1863 address is a plea for more attention to the education of the middle classes, but he also discusses the factory schools and echoes the criticisms made in Horner's reports. Marx must also have noticed a passage in which Senior praises 'the mixture of bodily and intellectual labour', recommends military drill for schools and adds that 'Mere bodily labour, though less efficient, is of great intellectual value' (Senior 1863, pp. 63–65).

By the time the first volume of *Capital* appeared, new controversies had broken out over part-time factory schools. Some claimed that the scheme was a failure. Others thought that it could still be made to work properly. Marx remained a strong supporter of the factory school. As late as 1875 he was rejecting demands for the abolition of child labour, this time as part of his sweeping rejection of the Gotha programme.

> Its implementation—if it were possible—would be reactionary, since, with a strict regulation of the working time according to the different age groups and other precautionary stipulations for the protection of children, an early combination of productive labour with education is one of the most potent means for the transformation of present-day society (Marx and Engels 1975–2005, vol. 24, p. 98).

The point seems to be a political one. In Marx's preferred system, children would certainly gain an awareness of the relation between wage labour and capital, but in the workplace, through their own experience, rather than in the classroom as some socialists proposed. But it was too late for this. In Britain, successive Elementary Education Acts had begun to make schooling compulsory for children, and similar legislation was being introduced in other advanced nations. Capitalism managed to survive the loss of a child workforce, despite Marx's claim that "A general prohibition of child labour is incompatible with the existence of large-scale industry and hence an empty, pious wish" (Marx and Engels 1975–2005, vol. 24, p. 98).

4.3 The Debate Over State Education

As Marx continued to look into educational issues, he realised that role of the state was a central issue for any future form of schooling. The resolution on children's work and education passed at the 1866 IWMA congress began with the regulation of child labour and the combination of work with schooling, and then put the case for using state power to establish public education. Marx knew that its audience would be suspicious of reliance on what they regarded as a power hostile to the working class. The policy argued that there were no available alternatives.

> The *right* of children and juvenile persons must be vindicated. They are unable to act for themselves. It is, therefore, the duty of society to act on their behalf.
>
> If the middle and higher classes neglect their duties toward their offspring, it is their own fault. Sharing the privileges of these classes, the child is condemned to suffer from their prejudices.
>
> The case of the working class stands quite different. The working man is no free agent. In too many cases, he is even too ignorant to understand the true interest of his child, or the normal conditions of human development. However, the more enlightened part of the working class fully understands that the future of its class, and, therefore, of mankind, altogether depends upon the formation of the rising working generation. They know that, before everything else, the children and juvenile workers must be saved from the crushing effects of the present system. This can only be effected by converting *social reason* into *social force*, and, under given circumstances, there exists no other method of doing so, than through *general laws*, enforced by the power of the state. In enforcing such laws, the working class do not fortify governmental power. On the contrary, they transform that power, now used against them, into their own agency. They effect by one general act what they would vainly attempt by a multitude of isolated individual efforts (Marx and Engels 1975–2005, vol. 20, pp. 188–89).

The education resolution was not followed up at later IWMA congresses. Other issues were more pressing and controversial. Several involved conflict between Marx's supporters and those of Proudhon in France and Lassalle in Germany. Schooling was not on the agenda of the 1867 Lausanne congress. In Brussels the following year the Third Congress threw up its hands, declaring that 'it is impossible at present to organise a rational system of education' and suggesting that sections should offer public lectures for workers (Documents of the First

International 1868–1870 1964, p. 294). A month before the Fourth Congress began in Basel in 1869, the issue was raised again at a meeting of the IWMA General Council in London. The secretary's minutes record a lively discussion, with Marx making a lengthy contribution in response to opinions expressed by other members.

Johann Eccarius, a veteran of the Communist League, opened the topic by suggesting that the Geneva resolution needed to determine 'whose business it was to look after the education and who would provide the means. As there was a difficulty in raising a large amount of taxes there were no other means but to take it out of the standing army and the established church. The reason why the last two congresses had come to no resolution was because many, particularly the French, objected to entrust the matter to the state' (Documents of the First International 1868–1870 1964, p. 140). This was only one theme in the debate that followed. Marx took the opportunity to restate the themes of the 1866 policy at some length, emphasising the need for working within the existing social order, while at the same time arguing against (as he later put it) education 'by the state'.

> Citizen Marx said there was a peculiar difficulty connected with this question. On the one hand change of social circumstances was required to establish a proper system of education, on the other hand a proper system of education was required to bring about a change of social circumstances; we must therefore commence where we were.
>
> The question treated at the congresses was whether education was to be national or private. National education had been looked upon as governmental, but that was not necessarily the case. In Massachusetts every township was bound to provide schools for primary education for all the children. In towns of more than 5,000 inhabitants higher schools for technical education had to be provided, in larger towns still higher. The state contributed something but not much. In Massachusetts one-eighth of the local taxes went for education, in New York one-fifth. The school committees who administered the schools were local, they appointed the schoolmasters and selected the books. The fault of the American system was that it was too much localised, the education given depended upon the state of culture prevailing in each district. There was a cry for a central supervision. The taxation for schools was compulsory, but the attendance of children was not. Property had to pay the taxes and the people who paid the taxes wanted that the money was usefully applied.
>
> Education might be national without being governmental. Government might appoint inspectors whose duty it was to see that the laws were obeyed, just as the factory inspectors looked after the observance of the factory acts, without any power of interfering with the course of education itself (Marx and Engels 1975–2005, vol. 21, p. 398).

This is Marx's most extended statement on education policy. It begins with what is, in effect, a restatement of the problem addressed by the third Thesis on Feuerbach. Marx does not specify his solution to the dilemma here, but only offers the rather obvious advice to 'begin where we are'. His main argument centres on a distinction between 'national' and 'governmental' education, citing as an example of the first option the decentralised public school system of Massachusetts. Noting some drawbacks in local control, he finally opts for a system of state regulation without 'interference', appealing to the established model of the British factory inspectors whose work he admired.

As he explains it here, Marx's approach to state education is designed to steer a course between two extremes of central control and excessive local variation. However careful his formulation was, it was soon overtaken by an outbreak of new controversies within the organisation. Towards the end of the 1860s, Marx's leadership was threatened by the Russian Mikhail Bakunin, defender of an anarchist philosophy strongly opposed to any participation in political representation within the existing state structures. Marx's rivalry with Bakunin was partly driven by national differences. For Bakunin, Marx was a typical Prussian (in fact a Rhinelander, historically something rather different). Conversely, Marx had a dislike for Russian autocracy, which he saw as an evil influence in European politics and an expansionist empire in Asia. 'The Russian bear is certainly capable of anything, so long as he knows the other animals he has to deal with to be capable of nothing' (Marx and Engels 1975–2005, vol. 12, p. 167).

Formed in 1868, Bakunin's organisation, the Geneva-based International Alliance of Socialist Democracy, set out to take over the IWMA by first gaining control of its Swiss and French sections. It took several years for Marx to bring about the final expulsion of Bakunin and his supporters, and by then the organisation was badly damaged. Its headquarters were moved to New York in an attempt to get away from European disputes, but new splits occurred and the association ended its life in 1874. In an 1872 article entitled 'Political Indifferentism', Marx took direct aim at Bakunin's insistence that workers should not participate in existing political process or rely on the existing state for support—including public education. As he mockingly puts it,

> It is better that working men and working women should not be able to read or write or do sums than that they should receive education from a teacher in a school run by the state. It is far better that ignorance and a working day of sixteen hours should debase the working classes than that eternal principles should be violated (Marx and Engels 1975–2005, vol. 23, p. 392).

Even so, Marx and Engels retained a suspicion of existing political structures. They were deeply impressed by the short-lived Paris Commune of 1870. At the General Council, Marx praised the Commune as a democratically elected body, composed mainly of working men, serving short terms and answerable to the people they represented. He thought that this confirmed that a socialist revolution could not simply take over existing state power but would have to set up an entirely new apparatus of government.

A main area of reform under the Commune was education. While it did not last long enough to establish a new kind of school, it had appointed a commission to reorganise primary and technical education. School teachers would be supplied by local government with books, maps and other tools of instruction to be used by their pupils without payment (Marx and Engels 1975–2005, vol. 22, p. 473). Marx emphasised that the Commune had enacted many of the policies supported by the IWMA. It had abolished the standing army and police, as well as depriving the Catholic Church of its privileged social position and its control of education.

> The whole of the educational institutions were opened to the people gratuitously, and at the same time cleared of all interference of church and state. Thus, not only was education made accessible to all, but science itself freed from the fetters which class prejudice and governmental force had imposed upon it (Marx and Engels 1975–2005, vol. 22, p. 332).

Marx added that a large section of the Paris middle class had endorsed the secularisation of education, a fact that he attributed to their 'Voltairianism'.

By the 1870s two German socialist parties had gained parliamentary representation: the pioneering General Association of German Workers founded by Ferdinand Lassalle in 1864 and its smaller rival, the IWMA-affiliated Social Democratic Workers' Party established in 1869 by August Bebel and Wilhelm Liebknecht. In 1875 the two organisations came together to form a united Socialist Workers' Party (renamed Social Democratic Party in 1890). The merger was negotiated at a conference in Gotha (*The Gotha programme* 1875). Marx was given a draft version of the joint political programme and responded with a lengthy polemic, later published as 'Notes on the Gotha programme'. He was vexed to see that even though his old rival Ferdinand Lassalle had been dead for a decade, his influence was still evident in the new party's programme, especially in its call for the use of the existing state in the interests of the working class.

Engels had launched a pre-emptive strike against expressions such as 'people's state' and 'free state' before the Gotha congress, writing to Bebel:

> Now, since the state is merely a transitional institution of which use is made in the struggle, in the revolution, to keep down one's enemies by force, it is utter nonsense to speak of a free people's state; so long as the proletariat still makes use of the state, it makes use of it, not for the purpose of freedom but of keeping down its enemies, and as soon as there can be any question of freedom, the state as such ceases to exist. We would therefore suggest that *Gemeinwesen* be universally substituted for *state*: it is a good old German word that can very well do service for the French 'Commune' (Marx and Engels 1975–2005, vol. 45, p. 64).

The model of the Paris Commune did not strike the German socialists as fitting their political situation, and so the 'free state' slogan remained in the draft programme. This aroused Marx's wrath. At best, he retorted, it could refer to relatively advanced societies of the present time, that is democratic republics such as Switzerland or the United States, which might seem to represent the future by German standards, but are just 'the last form of state of bourgeois society'. He returned to the same theme in commenting on the demand for 'Universal and equal education by the state'.

> '*Education of the people by the state*' is altogether objectionable. Defining by a general law the expenditures on the elementary schools, the qualifications of the teaching staff, the subjects of instruction, etc., and, as is done in the United States, supervising the fulfilment of these legal specifications by state inspectors, is a very different thing from appointing the state as the educator of the people! Government and Church should rather be equally excluded from any influence on the school. Particularly, indeed, in the Prusso-German Empire (and one should not take refuge in the rotten subterfuge that one is speaking of a 'state of the future'; we have seen how matters stand in this respect) the state has need, on the contrary, of a very stern education by the people (Marx and Engels 1975–2005, vol. 24, p. 97).

Despite Marx's protests, not made public at the time, the draft programme was approved at the Gotha conference. In later years it was left to Engels to uphold the ideal of a future society without any recognisable state—a defiant attempt, perhaps, to retain some element of the old utopian vision within an otherwise reformist set of political policies.

4.4 The Debate Over the Curriculum

After dealing with the issue of state support for education, the 1866 IWMA policy gets down to the task of designing a basic curriculum for the new school that it wants to create for the children of the working class.

> By education we understand three things.
> Firstly: *Mental education*.
> Secondly: *Bodily education*, such as is given in schools of gymnastics, and by military exercise.
> Thirdly: *Technological training*, which imparts the general principles of all processes of production, and, simultaneously initiates the child and young person in the practical use and handling of the elementary instruments of all trades. A gradual and progressive course of mental, gymnastic, and technological training ought to correspond with the classification of the juvenile workers. The costs of the technological schools ought to be partly met by the sale of the products. The combination of paid productive labour, mental education, bodily exercise and polytechnic training, will raise the working class far above the level of the higher and middle classes (Marx and Engels 1975–2005, vol. 20, p. 189).

What is meant by 'mental education' here? Surprisingly, the answer might be something not far removed from the *Examine*r that Eleanor Marx named as her most detested 'vice'. At least, this is consistent with what Marx says in the General Council's 1869 discussion. After he had reaffirmed the main points of the policy, George Milner, representing the National Reform Association, which campaigned for universal male suffrage, made a proposal for a further addition: 'the working class ought to insist that with production the children ought to learn the laws that regulate the value of the produce of labour' (Documents of the First International 1868–1870 1964, p. 141). Seeing trouble coming, Hermann Jung, the Swiss watchmaker who was Marx's most dependable supporter on the Council, moved the adjournment of the debate until the next meeting.

A week later, the discussion of education was resumed. Jung opened by expressing views similar to Marx's, emphasising the need for compulsory education within the present state of society, despite class divisions. He gave America and Switzerland as examples of successful systems of public education. According to the minutes, 'He disagreed with Cit. Milner. Who should give the education to instruct children as to the value of labour? There was a great difference of opinion as to what that value consisted of… He was opposed to any theories being introduced into the school. He would like to know what Cit. Milner meant'. In response, Milner repeated that 'the question of value and distribution' should be included in the school curriculum. He was supported by the Chartist George Harris, who complained that 'the agricultural labourer knew nothing of the value of his labour'.

In the debate that followed, Johann Eccarius 'observed that the value of labour was estimated differently by the two great classes of society'. Another member, whose name was not recorded in the minutes (possibly Milner again) 'could not accept that the value of labour was an accident. An hour's labour of one man was an equivalent for an hour's labour of another man, that must be impressed upon the rising generation. Warren in America had shown what equitable commerce was' (Documents of the First International 1868–1870 1964, p. 146).

Marx must have heard this last assertion with some exasperation. He was familiar with the principle of 'equitable commerce' and had been arguing against it for twenty years, in *The Poverty of Philosophy* and public lectures. In draft writings of the 1850s he devoted many pages to attacking the utopian scheme of 'time-money' based on the idea that an hour of one person's labour is worth as much an hour of another person's labour. Any such scheme, he insisted, was unworkable as long as labour was directed towards the production of commodities. Just as annoyingly, four years earlier Marx had addressed the General Council on the subject of wages, arguing that a general rise in wages would reduce the rate of profit, but would not harm workers by raising the prices of commodities, as some had claimed (Marx and Engels 1975–2005, vol. 20, pp. 101–49). He wrote to Engels before the session that dealt with this proposal:

> Of course I know beforehand what the two main points are: 1) that *wages* determine the value of commodities; 2) that if the capitalists pay 5 instead of 4 shillings today, they will sell their commodities for 5 instead of 4 shillings tomorrow (being enabled to do so by the increased demand). Inane though this is, attaching itself only to the most superficial external appearance, it is nevertheless not easy to explain to ignorant people all the economic questions which compete with one another here. You can't compress a course of political economy into one hour. But we shall do our best (Marx and Engels 1975–2005, vol. 41, p. 159).

The 'Warren' that Milner referred to was Josiah Warren, the American advocate of cooperation, who believed that it was possible to teach children the principles of fairness in social interactions. In his book *Equitable Commerce*, published in 1852, Warren gave an example of such instruction. 'My little daughter was between seven and eight years old when I commenced the application of these principles to her education'. He describes a conversation with his daughter.

> "You know that you eat and drink every day, that you have clothes, that you live in a house, that you sit by the fire, have books, playthings, attendance when you are sick, etc.; and yet, you cannot make any kind of food, you cannot make any part of your clothing—no part of the house you live in, nor the fire-wood; these must be made for you by others, and how do you get them? Do you know how you get them?" "I get them from you and mother," said she (Warren 1965, p. 110).

The father now explains that society works by a division of labour. Different people do different things, and then engage in exchange—not just of things, but of ideas and feelings as well. Even so, exchange is often badly and unfairly organised. Hence, his task is to put things right. Coming back to the family, he suggests that if each parent works three hours a day for the child, it is only fair that she should work the same amount of time for them.

> We agreed that from between seven and nine, from twelve to two, and from five till seven, should be the six hours of each day to be devoted to our work, and that all the rest of her time was to be entirely her own; and if we required her services during any of this time, we would make a contract with her as with any stranger, and pay her by the time employed, and the pay was to be absolutely her own, of which she was to be supreme sovereign disposer (Warren 1965, p. 112).

What strikes the modern reader is Warren's impersonal conception of family relations. Such a levelling of human relationships is common amongst utopian thinkers. 'If there is ever to be undisturbed harmony between parents and children', Warren writes, 'it will be found where their interests and responsibilities are entirely *individualized, disconnected* from each other, where one exercises no power or authority over the persons, property, time, or responsibilities of the other' (Warren 1965, p. 113).

Marx does not comment on this aspect, but he certainly rejects the content of Warren's lesson, as well as the 'labour time system' based on the same principle. He is less critical of Robert Owen's use of this concept, because Owen is not speaking of labour aimed at producing commodities. He even speculates that in the initial stages of a future socialist society, some such system could be used (Marx and Engels 1975–2005, vol. 24, p. 86). But an accurate account of the value of labour within a capitalist system of production would not be possible to supply to children of school age.

Marx tried to explain this to the General Council in his talks on the theory of wages, effectively an outline of the model soon to appear in *Capital*. 'There exists no such thing as the value of labour in the common sense of the word', he asserts (Marx and Engels 1975–2005, vol. 20, p. 128). Or as he puts it in *Capital*, 'Labour is the substance, and the immanent measure of value, but has itself no value' (Marx and Engels 1975–2005, vol. 35, p. 537). Yet Marx does not think that 'the value of labour' is a meaningless phrase. He rejects Proudhon's claim that it is 'a figurative expression' and that only the objects produced by labour really possess value (Marx and Engels 1975–2005, vol. 6, p. 129). If that were so, Marx responds, a simple change in language would dispel the error. In fact, 'the value of labour' is an expression that accurately describes the inevitable appearance of things in a capitalist system, and so covers up a 'grim reality', the reality of the expropriation that in Marx's terminology consists in the presence of surplus labour in the outcome of the sale of labour power.

It would have been impossible to go over this ground again at the 1869 meeting. Instead, Marx adopted a different strategy, moving to separate the whole issue from education policy.

> Citizen Milner's proposition was not suitable to be introduced in connection with the schools; it was a kind of education that the young must get from the adults in the everyday struggle of life. He could not accept Warren as a bible, it was a question upon which few

could agree. We might add that such education cannot be given at school, but must be given by adults.

Nothing could be introduced either in primary or higher schools that admitted of party and class interpretation. Only subjects such as the physical sciences, grammar, etc., were fit matter for schools. The rules of grammar, for instance, could not differ, whether explained by a religious Tory or a free thinker. Subjects that admitted of different conclusions must be excluded and left for the adults to such teachers as Mrs Law, who gave instruction in religion (Marx and Engels 1975–2005, vol. 21, pp. 399–400).

Of course, Marx did not think that different conclusions were equally valid. Nor did Harriet Law, a prominent member of the National Secular Society and frequent lecturer on the harm done by established religion. In her contribution to the debate, Mrs Law suggested that all Church property and income be confiscated and used for public schools. Marx was reluctant to see the socialist movement identified with rejection of religious belief, even if most socialists were not members of any Christian denomination. This was a later point of contention with Bakunin and his followers, who were militant atheists. Still, he endorsed a separation between the church and the public schools.

4.5 Polytechnical Education

So far, Marx's proposed curriculum does not look very different from conventional schooling. It begins with 'mental education' and then adds 'bodily education', explained as a combination of gymnastics and military exercise. After that comes a completely different element. In this document it is called 'technological training', but since the expression 'polytechnical education' later became more common, that will be used here. It is spelled out as a training which 'imparts the general principles of all processes of production, and, simultaneously initiates the child and young person in the practical use and handling of the elementary instruments of all trades.' This is the programme's most striking suggestion, and it shows Marx's ability to bring together various traditions of educational thought in a single conception.

First of all, the concept of *Bildung* is an inescapable background influence (Small 2005, pp. 109–12). It is true that a practical training in technology looks very different from a classical education. Yet when one goes deeper, a common element emerges. Both approaches emphasise all-round human development and reject narrow specialisation, especially with a vocational orientation. Both imply a humanistic philosophy and moral psychology, without appeals to metaphysical doctrines or religious beliefs. Further, both define their aim as addressing the needs not only of the individual person but also of social groups, and even whole societies. In his early writing on the theme of alienation, Marx had drawn on the humanistic critique of modern society, identifying private property as the real source of harm to the wholeness of the individual person. In *Capital* he returns to the subject from a consideration of the division of labour or, rather, of its form within the capitalist mode of production. Yet he still calls on the tradition of *Bildung*, citing one of its philosophical representatives, G. W. F. Hegel: 'By well educated men (*gebildeten Menschen*) we understand, in the first instance, those who can do everything that others do' (Marx and Engels 1975–2005, vol. 35, p. 368 referring to Hegel 1952, p. 268).

At the same time, Marx is aware of a parallel emphasis on many-sided human activity in the tradition of socialist thought, especially in utopian visions of a community in which people are no longer imprisoned within limited social roles. In *The German Ideology* Marx and Engels speculate on daily life in a society that has abolished class divisions:

> ... in communist society, where nobody has one exclusive sphere of activity but each can become accomplished in any branch he wishes, society regulates the general production and thus makes it possible for me to do one thing today and another tomorrow, to hunt in the morning, fish in the afternoon, rear cattle in the evening, criticise after dinner, just as I have a mind, without ever becoming hunter, fisherman, shepherd or critic (Marx and Engels 1975–2005, vol. 5, p. 47).

This is plainly an idealised image, but the crucial point is made: people's lives should not be confined to narrow occupational categories. The question now is: how can we relate such an idyllic vision to a world in which production is carried out by manufacture and industry? Hunting, fishing and rearing cattle may still go on, but they provide employment for only a few people, or are engaged in only as personal pastimes. What is crucial here is the modern division of labour, and the particular form it takes within a capitalist system.

For this reason, Marx draws mainly on political economists such as Adam Smith and Adam Ferguson, whose analysis of modern production centres on an increased division of labour and resulting specialisation of working life. They see this as an indispensable means of progress, particularly in increasing social prosperity. At the same time, they draw attention to the effects on the individual of excessive specialisation, accusing it of turning out fragmented and one-sided human beings. Yet the political economists seldom suggest solutions. Adam Smith advocates public education as promoting the common good, but only because it makes the common people 'more decent and orderly' and 'less apt to be misled into any wanton or unnecessary opposition to the measures of government' (Smith 1937, p. 740). Marx, in contrast, insists that education must address the human problems posed by excessive specialisation.

> What characterizes the division of labour in the automatic workshop is that labour has there completely lost its specialised character. But the moment every special development stops, the need for universality, the tendency towards an integral development of the individual begins to be felt. The automatic workshop wipes out specialists and craft-idiocy (Marx and Engels 1975–2005, vol. 6, p. 190).

Marx is aware that the word 'idiot' in ancient Greek means something like 'isolation'. In his view, a very specialised, narrowly trained individual is somebody who is cut off from the rest of the human race. So the elimination of traditional craft occupations is an advance, because it enables us to think, possibly for the first time since such skills originally arose, about the development of all-round capacities. And in this Marx sees the opportunity for an all-round education.

He found strong support for this general idea in Claude-Anthime Corbon's book *De l'enseignement professionnel*, published in 1859 and read by Marx soon afterwards in the British Museum. The author was a French politician, liberal rather than socialist, with an interest in working-class education. In this short work intended to promote technical schooling, Corbon—a skilled woodworker as well as printer in his youth—argues that manual trades are not as hard to learn as people imagine. They tend to involve skills that more or less fall into two general categories: those requiring precise workmanship according to set rules, such as carpentry, stone cutting and tailoring, and those requiring imagination and individual flair, such as jewellery and decorative painting or sculpting. Within these broad divisions, any young person should be capable of picking up more than one trade, given the opportunity.

Corbon goes on to argue that modern society needs versatile people who can move between different branches of industry during their working lives. Great inventors of the Industrial Revolution such as James Watt, Richard Arkwright and Robert Fulton all began their working lives in traditional trades. If they had been guided by advice to 'mind their own business', we would not have the steam engine, spinning machine or steamboat. With this in mind, we need to rethink the idea of technical education. It should provide training for young future workers in the tools of various occupations, starting as early as possible but postponing actual entry into the workforce until the age of 15 years (Corbon 1859, p. 131). Corbon is not convinced that the existing institutions calling themselves technical schools are achieving this goal. Hence, he advocates government action to make technical education available to a much wider group of young people.

Marx spends several pages in *Capital* repeating Corbon's arguments, and borrows his list of inventors who transformed production by thinking outside the limits of their original occupations (Marx and Engels 1975–2005, vol. 35, p. 491). Otherwise he is selective. He is not interested in Corbon's suggestions for establishing technical schools in rural areas. His concern is the children of the urban working class. He assumes that they are not going to attend university or enter professional occupations, but will be wage labourers in workshops, offices and factories. He is also aware that technical education is already in existence, but wants to emphasise that this is not what he has in mind. The General Council minutes report him as saying:

> The technological training advocated by proletarian writers was meant to compensate for the deficiencies occasioned by the division of labour which prevented apprentices from acquiring a thorough knowledge of their business. This had been taken hold of and misconstructed [*sic*] into what the middle class understood by technical education (Marx and Engels 1975–2005, vol. 21, p. 399).

Elsewhere he explains what he thinks the reasons are for the provision of public education within the capitalist system of production. 'The true purpose which education has with the philanthropic economists is this: every worker should be trained in as many industries as possible, so that if by the introduction of new machines or by a change in the division of labour he is thrown out of one industry, he can as easily as possible find employment in another' (Marx and Engels 1975–2005, vol. 6, p. 427). In that case, a ready supply of labour for new or expanding branches of production will ensure that wages can be kept from rising there.

So capitalism has its own reasons for accepting that mass schooling is a necessary part of modern society. In *Capital*, Marx concludes his analysis of machinery and heavy industry by emphasising the positive side of the flexibility it imposes on workers. They can move from one branch of industry to another as desired, rather than spending their lives in 'life-long repetition of one and the same trivial operation'. Then he turns to education:

> One step already taken spontaneously towards effecting this revolution is the establishment of technical and agricultural schools (*polytechnische und agronomische Schulen*), and of *écoles d'enseignement professionnel*, in which the children of the workingmen receive some little instruction in technology and in the practical handling of the various implements of labour. Though the Factory Act, that first and meagre concession wrung from capital, is limited to combining elementary education with work in the factory, there can be no doubt that when the working class comes into power, as inevitably it must, technical instruction (*technologischen Unterricht*), both theoretical and practical, will take its proper place in the working-class schools (Marx and Engels 1975–2005, vol. 35, p. 491).

Here Marx has in mind French rather than British education, probably owing to his reading of Corbon. He is referring to *grandes écoles,* such as the *École polytechnique* and *Institut national agronomique*, parallel to universities but providing instruction in technical subjects.

In the French edition of *Capital*, closely supervised by Marx and including some rewriting on his part, this passage takes on a sharper tone. 'The bourgeoisie which, in creating polytechnical and agronomic, etc., schools for its sons, was merely obeying the inner tendencies of modern production, has given the proletarians only the shadow of *enseignement professionnel*'. Further, after 'elementary education' he inserts 'miserable as it may be' (Marx 1872–75, p. 211). Evidently Marx felt that he had presented these developments too uncritically. Now he separates the professional training of technicians and engineers from a vocational schooling for future tradesmen and skilled labourers, and emphasises how little education will be provided to workers by a ruling class that has only its own interests in mind.

Marx certainly wants an 'education of the future', suitable for a society not divided into classes. He believes that this education can exist already within a capitalist society, at least in some 'embryonic' form. Hence, his qualified endorsement of the trend towards *enseignement professionnel,* and his proposal for a school which will eventually 'raise the working class far above the level of the higher and middle classes'. Still, the complexity of his position is not always evident. Consider one apparently straightforward remark. John Bellers, he says, 'saw most clearly at the end of the 17th century, the necessity for abolishing the present system of education' (Marx and Engels 1975–2005, vol. 35, p. 491). The key word in Marx's German text is *Aufhebung*. Translating this as 'abolishing' is often quite correct. However, we need to remember that Marx's intellectual background is Hegelian thought, where the word *Aufhebung* is valued highly as combining meanings which contradict each other and yet, when taken together, characterise a process that is at the heart of philosophical thinking. Since there is no English equivalent, some translators of Hegel have resorted to a novel term, 'sublate', as in the following passage from Hegel's *Science of Logic*:

> 'To sublate' has a twofold meaning in the language: on the one hand it means to preserve, to maintain and equally it also means to cause to cease, to put an end to. Even 'to preserve' contains a negative element, namely, that something is removed from its immediacy and so from an existence which is open to external influences, in order to preserve it (Hegel 1969, p. 107).

Hegel goes on to explain that 'something is sublated only in so far as it has entered into unity with its opposite'. We get a preview here of the simplified formula of thesis, antithesis and synthesis that came to be used in the later Marxian tradition.

All this is relevant to an adequate reading of Marx's comment on Bellers. When he speaks of the need to 'abolish' the present system of education, what he means is that the school should take on a new form by entering into unity with what is now its opposite—that is the world of productive labour. That is just what the IWMA's proposals for combining work and schooling, and for polytechnical training in schools, are designed to bring about: to bring that world into the daily life of the school. Marx may not have placed himself in the movement for child-centred education, but he could endorse John Dewey's view that 'Education is a process of living and not a preparation for future living' (Dewey 1897).

References

Bellers, J. (1695). *A Proposal for raising a colledge of industry of all useful trades and husbandry, with profit for the rich, a plentiful living for the poor, and a good education for youth which will be advantage to the government, by the increase of the people, and their riches*. London: T. Sowle.

Corbon, C.-A. (1859). *De l'enseignement professionnel*. Paris: Imprimerie de Dubuisson et cie.

Dewey, J. (1897). *My Pedagogic creed*. http://en.wikisource.org/wiki/My_Pedagogic_Creed. Accessed 1 June 2013.

Documents of the First International 1868–1870. (1964). London: Lawrence and Wishart.

Eves, C., & Eves, G. (1852). *The school examiner*. London: Simpkin, Marshall and Co., Whittaker and Co.; Darton and Co.; Aylott and Jones; Relphe and Brothers; Law, Fleet Street; Bean, Hoxton; Harris, Hatton Garden; Harris, St John Street; Harris, Whitechapel; and the Authors, 73, Myddellton Street, Wilmington Square.

Eves, C., & Eves, G. (1854). *Key to the school examiner*. London: Relfe & Brothers; Darton & Co.; C.H. Law; Longman & Co.; Simpkin, Marshall & Co.; Whittaker & Co.; J. & C. Mozley, Derby. Oliver & Boyd, Edinburgh. McGlashan, Dublin. The Authors, 73, Myddellton Street, Wilmington Square.

The Gotha programme. (1875). http://history.hanover.edu/courses/excerpts/111gotha.html. Accessed 1 June 2013.

Hegel, G. W. F. (1952). *Philosophy of right* (trans: Knox, T. M.). Oxford: Clarendon Press.

Hegel, G. W. F. (1969). *Science of logic* (trans: Miller, A. V.). London: Allen and Unwin.

Marx, K. (1872–1875). *Le Capital*. (trans: Roy, J.) Paris: Maurice Lachatre.

Marx, K., Engels, F. (1975–2005). *Collected works*, (Vols. 50). London: Lawrence and Wishart.

Omura, I., Fomicev, V., Hecker, R., & Kuno, S. (Eds.). (2005). *Marx Familie privat: Die Photo- und Frage-Bogen Alben von Marx' Töchtern Laura und Jenny*. Berlin: Akademie Verlag.

Senior, N. W. (1844). *Letters on the Factory Act, as it affects the cotton manufacture, addressed, in the spring of 1837, to the Right Honourable the President of the Board of Trade* (2nd ed). London: B. Fellowes and J. Ridgeway.

Senior, N. W. (1863) *Address to the National Association for the promotion of social science. Report of Proceedings at the Seventh Annual Congress, Held in Edinburgh*, October 1863 (pp. 44–66) Edinburgh: William P. Nimmo, 1863.

Small, R. (2005). *Marx and education*. Aldershot: Ashgate.

Smith, A. (1937). *The wealth of nations*. New York: Modern Library.

Warren, J. (1852/1965). *Equitable commerce. A new development of principles as substitutes for laws and governments, for the harmonious adjustment and regulation of the pecuniary, intellectual, and moral intercourse of mankind proposed as elements of new society*. 1852; reprint ed., New York: Burt Franklin.

Chapter 5
Lessons from Marx

Abstract What can we learn from Marx about today's education? His analysis of capitalism provides clues for grasping the place of schooling in modern societies. On his view, the school is not simply an ideological institution, but is important in producing labour power. This involves passing on social knowledge, but by distributing it very unequally to different social groups, the school contributes to the reproduction of social relations. What about the situation of teachers in our society? Their position is under continual pressure from economic and political forces whose tendency is to impose the typical conditions of wage labour on their work, such as managerial control and standardised procedures designed to remove the need for individual judgement. Marx seems to dismiss the alternative idea of teaching as a professional occupation as outdated sentimentalism, and yet this model may serve as a means of resistance and a source of countervailing power for teachers.

Keywords Karl Marx • Education • Schooling • Ideology • Social knowledge • Public good • Unproductive labour • Professionalism

5.1 Introduction

In the twenty-first century, Marx is making a comeback. This is not because his political ideas are being adopted by governments across the world. On the contrary, they suffered for seventy years from association with the Soviet version of communism, whose final failure seemed to justify dismissing Marx from consideration. Yet a very different conclusion is now being drawn by many commentators. As Meghnad Desai puts it, 'in the triumphant resurgence of capitalism—and, indeed, its global reach—the one thinker who is vindicated is Karl Marx' (Desai 2002, p. 3). Similarly, in his book *Why Marx Was Right* Terry Eagleton writes: 'Marxism is a critique of capitalism—the most searching, rigorous, comprehensive

R. Small, *Karl Marx*, SpringerBriefs on Key Thinkers in Education,
DOI: 10.1007/978-94-007-7657-9_5,

critique of its kind ever to be launched... It follows, then, that as long as capitalism is still in business, Marxism must be as well' (Eagleton 2011, p. 2).

And capitalism is still in business. Some Marxists used to refer to 'late capitalism'. The implication was that the capitalist mode of production was nearer its end than its beginning. That claim remains to be confirmed. What was true in the label was a recognition that capitalism is always changing. The fact that it may not be thriving in the places where it first emerged is consistent with this protean character. Capital is restless, mobile and global in its outlook, as Marx and Engels point out in the *Communist Manifesto*. It has no loyalty to any homeland and no sentimentality over past history. Further, instability is part of its nature, as the financial and debt crises of the twenty-first century have reminded us.

Inevitably, then, this is the situation within which today's education must confront its problems. We have seen how Marx responded to the educational issues of his time. What would he say about ours? Or rather, what can we learn from him? Quite a lot, but only by bringing our own thinking to the task. Simply repeating what he says about the education of his time will not be enough. The establishment of public school systems throughout the Western world occurred towards the end of Marx's life, too late to be addressed in his writings. However successful or unsuccessful the part-time factory school may have been over the previous thirty years, it became irrelevant from then on. Even Marx's forward-looking idea of polytechnical training is not easy to relate to today's educational realities. Because our school systems did not exist when Marx was writing, he understandably felt free to draw on the appealing pictures of the education of the future drawn by utopian writers, despite his general suspicion of ideal visions.

When we go back to Marx's analysis of the capitalist mode of production and locate education within that framework, some contrasting features emerge. If his survey of the cultural achievements of capitalism had been written a few decades later, it could have included public education, despite his description of the educational provisions of the Factory Acts as a 'concession wrung from capital' (Marx and Engels 1975–2005, vol. 35, p. 491). The introduction of mass schooling as a function of the modern state is a consistent pattern in industrialised societies. Yet while capitalism demands public education, it also has a strong tendency to restrict its scope and content, as well as distributing access to its benefits very unevenly across social groups. So let us start by seeing how Marx identifies each of these powerful forces in his account of modern society.

Where workshop and factory labour is concerned, he assumes that capitalism can get by without providing much schooling for its working class. 'Adam Smith knew however how little "education" [Marx is writing in German but uses the English word] enters into the costs of production of the mass of working men' (Marx and Engels 1975–2005, vol. 31, p. 23). What about other kinds of wage earners? In the third volume of *Capital*, he discusses the position of office workers—clerks, sales assistants and so on—who do not produce surplus value directly, although they are needed to keep the overall system of production going. Their work is seen as skilled compared to manual labour, yet this does not necessarily bring them any economic advantage, for several reasons. The first is that further specialisation within the workplace reduces any need for training, 'since the labourer's skill develops by itself through the exercise of his function, and all the more rapidly as division of labour makes it more one-sided' (Marx and Engels 1975–2005, vol. 37, 299). The other reason is that the knowledge and skills which cannot readily be picked up on the job are provided at relatively little cost by public education.

> Secondly, because the necessary training, knowledge of commercial practices, languages, etc., is more and more rapidly, easily, universally and cheaply reproduced with the progress of science and public education (*Volksbildung*) the more the capitalist mode of production directs teaching methods, etc., towards practical purposes (Marx and Engels 1975–2005, vol. 37, p. 299).

These workers must have some knowledge to do their jobs, unlike unskilled labourers. However, Marx gives two reasons for doubting whether this demand translates into a higher price for their labour power. First, many specialised skills are acquired in carrying out the work, and so require no special training. Secondly, public education has become an efficient way of producing workers with literacy, numeracy and some general knowledge. One advantage for employers is that they need not bear the expense of training future workers. This cost is met by the parents who pay school fees or, as was soon to come about in the United Kingdom and other countries, by the state's provision of funding for schools of its own.

Marx adds another observation: that a capitalist system 'directs' schools towards a curriculum and pedagogy that aim at practical outcomes, not at any kind of personal development for its own sake. As well as teaching knowledge and work skills, the school is supposed to ensure that the new generation have habits and attitudes that fit them for employment in modern offices, workshops and factories. But how is this pressure exerted? In the modern world, through education policies imposed by state authority. These in turn are the outcome of political processes that, for Marx, need to be analysed in terms of class interests.

The passage quoted above goes on to give further reasons for the failure of white-collar workers to gain an economic benefit from an increased demand for their labour:

> The universality of public education (*Volksunterrichts*) makes it possible to recruit such labourers from classes that formerly had no access to such trades and were accustomed to a lower standard of living. Moreover, this increases supply, and hence competition. With few exceptions, the labour-power of these people is therefore devaluated with the progress of capitalist production (Marx and Engels 1975–2005, vol. 37, p. 299).

Here Marx points out another important feature of modern education: it enables some degree of social mobility, if not between one class and another, then at least towards jobs with better working conditions and higher wages. As before, rather than noting any positive aspects Marx predicts a harmful effect on wage levels owing to competition between workers. Yet he does not want to assert that the working class receives no benefit at all from schooling in its present form. After all, his own plan for a future school avoids the charge of utopianism by adapting and building on current realities. Further, in *Capital* he notes the establishment of technical and agricultural schools as 'one step already taken spontaneously' towards an education system corresponding to human needs in an industrial society (Marx and Engels 1975–2005, vol. 35, p. 491).

The word 'spontaneously' (*naturwüchsig*) is important. Capitalism is driven by its immediate needs, not by planning for the future, and so unforeseen consequences are inevitable. The most important of these, for Marx, is the creation of a working class that is capable of bringing about a transition to a new kind of society, one that does not rely on class domination. This is the context for his observations of existing forms of schooling, and for our use of his ideas for the current situation. The following discussion will focus on two central topics in which we can learn from Marx, by taking his ideas as our starting point. One is the place of the school in today's society. The other is the situation of the people whose working lives are spent in this school—that is, the teaching force. Of course, these are just two sides of the same issue. Why are capitalist societies caught in a double bind, needing their public education systems and yet driven to impose pressures that undermine their position and make a damaging impact on teachers and their work? Marx's analysis of the capitalist mode of production gives us directions for addressing this inescapable question.

5.2 Are Schools Ideological Institutions?

Describing the origins of modern society in *Capital*, Marx writes: 'The advance of capitalist production develops a working class, which by education, tradition, habit, looks upon the conditions of that method of production as self-evident laws of Nature' (Marx and Engels 1975–2005, vol. 35, p. 726). We can read this as identifying three ways in which the beliefs and attitudes of the working class are formed. The first is education, which since the late nineteenth century has meant compulsory schooling for all children. So let us consider the idea that one function of the modern school is to support and maintain the social status quo by imposing an ideological view of society on the new generation.

What does Marx think? He is certainly suspicious of any school curriculum devised by representatives of the middle class, especially where values are concerned: 'by moral education the bourgeois understands indoctrination with bourgeois principles' (Marx and Engels 1975–2005, vol. 6, p. 427). His 1866 plan for the school attempts to guard against that danger. When arguing that 'mental education' should be restricted to 'subjects such as the physical sciences, grammar, etc.', he draws attention to possible political and religious biases on the part of teachers. On the other hand, the *Communist Manifesto*'s response to the charge that it is turning education into something political by taking it away from the home is to assert that education is already political.

> But, you say, we destroy the most hallowed of relations, when we replace home education by social. And your education! Is not that also social, and determined by the social conditions under which you educate, by the intervention, direct or indirect, of society, by means

of schools, &c.? The Communists have not invented the intervention of society in education; they do but seek to alter the character of that intervention, and to rescue education from the influence of the ruling class (Marx and Engels 1975–2005, vol. 6, pp. 501–502).

Marx is aware of the social influences that enter into education, whether their presence is acknowledged or not, and sees the need to counteract them. This is a more realistic approach than any attempt to restrict the school curriculum to subjects that are supposedly protected from ideological influences by their formal and abstract character. Nowadays pressures to narrow the scope of education to 'basics' typically come from the forces that, as Marx observes, want teaching to serve 'practical purposes'—where that is understood with the interests of some groups but not others in mind.

What about the other two influences that Marx mentions, 'tradition' and 'habit'? Both are present within the daily practices of the school, but in other places as well. The family is especially relevant to education, because children come into the school with attitudes and beliefs already formed in the home. Other aspects of life in a community—religion, accepted morality and custom—bring with them established ways of thinking and behaving. Finally, there are the experiences of everyday life, especially in the workplace, which has its own habitual practices and taken-for-granted attitudes, arising in spontaneous and unconsidered ways rather than from the employer's directions. (In fact, these may be forms of resistance to that authority and control.)

Tradition and habit are hard to pin down, since they may be hidden or dispersed across various locations. So let us focus on education, and ask whether Marx is right in hinting that one of the school's functions (not necessarily the only one) is to turn out a working class that takes the norms of the capitalist system to be 'self-evident laws of nature'. It helps to have a general label for such beliefs, and his thought provides one: 'ideology'. Now the question becomes: are schools ideological institutions?

We have seen that Marx sets out in *Capital* to explain why false ideas about the capitalist mode of production are so common. He compares the contrast between the semblance of fair exchange and the reality of appropriated surplus value with an object's surface and its interior. The point is that the surface is what we see—in fact, it is all that we normally see. In this case the full account is more complex, since it involves continual movement back and forth between the realms of circulation and production—that is, the metaphorical 'surface' and 'inside'. Summing up, Marx says that when we take this system to be operating by the rules of free exchange, 'we are subject to a mere illusion, though a necessary one' (Marx and Engels 1975–2005, vol. 28, p. 433). Such an illusion is not just in the mind; it is a feature of the situation. The semblance persists, even when one knows what is happening (Small 2005, p. 74). This insight helps us to get away from the notion of ideology as a false story that some people have managed to get others to believe. If that were true, overcoming it would be a lot easier. We could expose the lies and point out the truth. Things are not that simple, because ideologies are not simply deceptions imposed on some passive audience. They are grounded in experience, and this is the source of their strength and persistence.

Keeping this in mind, we can avoid the simplistic view that public education in capitalist society is an elaborate conspiracy to spread false beliefs. At the same time, what Marx says about the bourgeois notion of moral education is borne out by the school curriculum of that time, designed to promote obedience and conformity by means of religious and patriotic values. Anyone looking at *Eves's Examiner* will be struck by its value content. So the school does provide opportunities for indoctrination. With compulsory attendance it has a captive audience and plenty of time to spend on achieving this aim. But one must remember that Marx located education within 'practical social relations' rather than with art, religion and philosophy in the higher regions of the social 'superstructure'. In that sense, any comparison with the Christian church is misleading. The school makes a far more practical and material contribution to maintaining the capitalist mode of production. As Marx puts it, 'education produces labour capacity' (Marx and Engels 1975–2005, vol. 31, p. 104). While the school may be a location where ideology is passed on, that is not its main function.

Hence, the question about the school's position in modern society remains to be answered. If Marx is right, the place to look for a clearer understanding is in its dynamic relation to the economic 'base', a two-way process of interaction. Now another element in the social 'superstructure' needs to be integrated into the account: the modern state. It may seem that the question of the state's role in education, an ongoing vexation for Marx's thinking about schooling, was resolved by the establishment of state education systems in capitalist countries. In fact, the school's relation to the state is still very unsettled, and so it must figure in any further discussion.

5.3 The State and the Privatisation of Knowledge

In recent times, expressions such as 'knowledge economy' and 'information society' have arisen. No doubt they are often used as slogans rather than concepts. Still, there is an idea here: that specialised knowledge and expertise is a crucial factor in the creation of new wealth, as well as being a commodity itself, from which commercial profit can be made. As it happens, Marx has some relevant points to make. In one draft for *Capital*, he speaks of the 'general intellect' or 'social mind'—that is, the sum of society's scientific understanding and expertise—as being a means of production in its own right when it gives rise to technology, and especially modern machinery (Marx and Engels 1975–2005, vol. 29, pp. 92 and 84). Under capitalism, this applied knowledge belongs to the machine's owner, not to the worker, for whom it is an unknown, alien power. Whereas the traditional craftsman used tools in the labour process, now it is the machine that uses the worker, 'as a mere living accessory'. Thus, the scientific knowledge that should properly be the common heritage of humanity is 'absorbed into capital' as its own means of reproduction and growth. As Marx puts it, the general progress and accumulation of society's knowledge 'is appropriated gratis by capital' (Marx and Engels 1975–2005, vol. 29, p. 84).

Where does all this knowledge come from? Marx takes its source to be society in general, but he notes that, under capitalism, its growth is not left to chance: 'At this point, invention becomes a business, and the application of science to immediate production itself becomes a factor determining and soliciting science' (Marx and Engels 1975–2005, vol. 29, p. 90). Just as capitalism 'directs' public education in a vocational direction, so too it encourages and promotes scientific research of the kind that best suits its own purpose—that is, which contributes to increased productivity and therefore to greater profits.

Institutionalised education is bound up with this development. It is where existing social knowledge is passed on to each new generation and, in the case of the university, where it is built up further through disciplinary research. But Marx's sharp comment about the appropriation of knowledge applies here. When education distributes knowledge very unequally to different classes, it turns what ought to be a public good—'social knowledge'—into private property. Yet the cost of maintaining and developing this asset is carried by the whole community, through the state's funding of education.

When knowledge is identified in economic language as a 'public good', this means that it differs from familiar commodities such as food and clothing by not being 'consumed' in the everyday sense. That is, it is not diminished or, putting it another way, the cost of its production is not increased, when it is shared amongst a greater number of people. In textbook terminology, it is not 'rivalrous'. Another standard characteristic of a 'public good' is that access to it cannot be restricted. That is, it is not 'excludable'. Commonly given examples (which are also 'non-rivalrous') are lighthouses, fireworks displays and national defence. Whether this second property can be attributed to knowledge is debatable. Ideas have a tendency to spread despite attempts to restrict or suppress them. These days, attempts to manage knowledge are undermined by information technologies that give everyone access to intellectual resources—a realisation of Marx and Engels' conception of a world culture in which 'The intellectual creations of individual nations become common property' (Marx and Engels 1975–2005, vol. 6, p. 488).

Even so, the advantages of knowledge to social groups that can monopolise it is a strong motivation for restricting access. The knowledge that comes from formal education, and cannot be acquired without structured teaching or training over a long period, is not available to everyone on an equal basis. There is no lack of evidence that schooling in its existing form gives some a far better chance than others of gaining admission to higher education and, in particular, to courses that lead to professional qualifications. This bias is arguably a kind of 'enclosure' that delivers what should be a public asset into private hands. Those who work in education are typically committed to a very different ideal, a version of the Enlightenment philosophy that makes the pursuit of knowledge a universal human imperative. But they are not free agents. The modern state exercises considerable control, both direct and indirect, over what they can achieve as educators. So let us look at this side of the issue: the role of the state in the privatisation of knowledge—and in particular, the power of government as exerted through education policy.

First of all, we need to correct a common misconception. One perennial myth of capitalism is that the system operates best with little or no state intervention. On the contrary, Marx argues, the early history of industrial capitalism shows a systematic reliance on state power, often exercised with outright violence (Marx and Engels 1975–2005, vol. 35, pp. 738–748). The most notorious case is the privatisation of public assets carried out in eighteenth century England through the 'laws of settlement' that Marx calls 'decrees of expropriation of the people' (Marx and Engels 1975–2005, vol. 35, p. 715). Large landowners were able to take possession of common land, consolidating landed property and displacing the rural population, who were forced into the new industrial towns to become wage labourers. He gives other examples as well. The rise of national debt or public credit enabled profit-making to remain in private hands, while liabilities become a collective responsibility. Here Marx points to the great banks, privately owned and yet operating with legal privileges and ready access to the state as a major borrower. Increased taxation is then needed to support the national debt and the expenses of empire. The preferred objects of taxation are the things most needed in everyday life, so that the burden falls across the entire community, rather than on those who receive the greatest benefit.

Not all of the examples given by Marx find exact counterparts in today's world. After all, he is describing the period when capitalism is engaged in a struggle to win social power, not to maintain a long established status quo. Still, some will seem familiar to anyone who follows the news. Nowadays policies of state support for privately owned business and finance are found throughout Western societies, and even more in their newer competitors, where large corporations are established and protected by state power, effectively discouraging competition and creating monopolies in key industries. Marx was acquainted with one example: the East India Company, privately owned but licensed by royal charter to operate with special privileges across vast territories in distant countries. Even when the Company lost its remaining functions in the wake of the Indian insurrection of the 1850s, it continued to be protected by the British parliament. As Marx explained to his American readers in an 1857 newspaper article, 'despite all fine distinctions, as soon as the East India Company is supplanted by the British Government its debt will be merged into the British debt. A further increase of the large national debt seems, therefore, one of the first financial consequences of the Indian Revolt' (Marx and Engels 1975–2005, vol. 15, p. 446). Anyone who thinks that government bailouts for private business are a novel feature of the capitalist system, or inconsistent with its operating principles, needs to look more closely at the historical record.

In classical liberalism, the state is presented as a kind of umpire who defines and enforces the rules of play in market competition. In today's capitalist societies, the state is openly presented as more like a trainer or coach who issues instructions on strategy and tactics, urges players on to greater competitiveness and backs up these interventions with threatened penalties. The outcome is a market which is 'free' only within more or less narrow boundaries. Public education has become an area where such a quasi-market is openly defended as a way of combining public funding with consumer choice of product and provider. The outcome is a systematic undermining of state school systems and the introduction of competing educational providers with the same access to public funding.

Marx's approach to all such political issues is to insist on identifying the class interests that underlie the slogans of public debate. As with the economic analysis of *Capital*, his strategy is to locate particular individuals and events within a broader context. For example, the two articles on 'The State of British Manufactures' that he wrote for the *New York Daily Tribune* in 1859 (Marx and Engels 1975–2005, vol. 16, pp. 190–196 and 206–210) cover similar ground to the passages in *Capital* that deal with the Factory Acts. Here Marx treats the problems of the factory schools as due to deliberate loopholes in the relevant legislation, the outcome of ongoing conflicts between the differing economic interests of landowners and industrialists. While drawing on the reports of the inspectors, he rejects their professed view that the system's failures were unforeseen by the parliament that established it. If he were commenting on today's government policies, Marx would take a similar view, and look at public education as an area where the underlying reality of class conflict is the key to understanding how and why the modern school has never succeeded in living up to its often stated ideal of equal educational opportunity for all children. And he would no doubt draw on and endorse the work of the commentators on education policy who take just this approach.

5.4 Teachers and Their Work

Apart from the situation of today's schools, another important area of educational debate is the position of teachers and educators. Once again, we need to start with the bigger picture. Marx notes the contributions of education to different kinds of labour. But if training is a factor in the production of labour power, does this give teaching a special status in comparison with other occupations? Teaching is itself a kind of work that requires training, and this already suggests that it should be treated as a special case. So where does teaching fit into the picture of modern society that Marx presents? This question can be sharpened by looking at his treatment of two kinds of work, for which he uses labels borrowed from the political economists: *productive* and *unproductive* labour. They are dealt with in the first volume of *Capital*, and at greater length in the material eventually published as *Theories of Surplus Value*.

But the issue needs to be understood properly. Marx is not simply asking whether teaching is productive labour or not. When he introduces the distinction, it is to identify what political economists like Adam Smith mean when they use these terms—which is not necessarily what they claim to mean. Marx is not a participant in the disputes between Smith and his critics. He is something different: a critical commentator. Hence, it is wrong to assume that he must have his own concepts of productive and unproductive labour, and that these might apply to other societies. In fact, this debate allows him to reaffirm his thesis that economic categories have a historical character—that is, their meaning is not given once and for all but developed in and through some particular historical context. Hence, if he asserts that one interpretation is the correct one, he does not mean 'correct' in a general, abstract sense, but as an expression of the social relations of capitalism.

It is with this agenda in mind that Marx analyses what others have written, starting with Adam Smith. He finds two distinct conceptions of productive labour in Smith's work. The point of the contrast is that one usage is carried over from older forms of production, which were concerned with use value rather than exchange value. On this view, labour is productive if it produces objects that keep their value and can be exchanged again. This however excludes 'personal services', where what is bought is just the work itself, not anything that can be sold again at a different time and place. On this criterion, teachers seem to be unproductive workers. But Marx queries the concept itself. As he points out, most products keep their use value and, therefore, their exchange value, only for a limited time. He notes that some have defended certain occupations from the accusation of being unproductive by arguing that they do produce something that has an ongoing existence—a claim that could be made for teachers as well, if their students acquire knowledge and skills that will be used later on. Such attempts to expand the scope of productive labour provoke Marx into satirical mockery. 'A philosopher produces ideas, a poet poems, a clergyman sermons, a professor compendia and so on. A criminal produces crimes' (Marx and Engels 1975–2005, vol. 30, p. 306). Anyone who works can be said to produce something, but 'intellectual production' amounts to very different things in different historical settings (Marx and Engels 1975–2005, vol. 31, p. 182). Hence, Marx concludes, this argument relies on what are only 'general superficial analogies and relations between intellectual and material wealth' (Marx and Engels 1975–2005, vol. 31, p. 183).

Adam Smith's other concept of productive labour corresponds to the capitalist mode of production and, to that extent, is seen by Marx as the truer concept. Here 'productive' means: giving rise to surplus value. Labour is productive in this sense when it serves the expansion of capital—that is, when it enables an employer to make a profit by selling what has been produced by the wage labourer (Marx and Engels 1975–2005, vol. 31, p. 8). Because this concept is defined by the social relations of production, the same kind of work can be either productive or unproductive, depending on its circumstances. Teaching is a case in point, as Marx explains:

> If we may take an example from outside the sphere of production of material objects, a schoolmaster is a productive labourer, when, in addition to belabouring the heads of his scholars, he works like a horse to enrich the school proprietor. That the latter has laid out his capital in a teaching factory, instead of in a sausage factory, does not alter the relation (Marx and Engels 1975–2005, vol. 35, p. 510).

He notes that 'there are many such educational factories in England' (Marx and Engels 1975–2005, vol. 34, p. 144). So let us consider the activity of teaching, when it occurs in this context, that is, when it is done for an employer who is investing capital in order to make a profit. Taking the work of actors for a theatrical entrepreneur as his example, Marx comments: ‘the fact that their purchaser cannot sell them to the public in the form of commodities but only in the form of the action itself would show that they are unproductive labours’ (Marx and Engels 1975–2005, vol. 31, p. 28). Yet they are certainly productive from the employer’s standpoint. So, is this purchaser buying the action itself and selling it for a higher price? No, for consider the theatre director who engages a singer for a season, not to perform but only to prevent her from appearing in a rival theatre (Marx and Engels 1975–2005, vol. 28, p. 212). Evidently what is bought there is just the capacity to work—in other words, the employee’s labour power. But that must also be true of the singers who do appear on stage, since their agreement with the employer is the same. So even if cases of service from which profit is made are untypical, they do match the favoured notion of productive labour.

What makes Smith’s version important for Marx is its emphasis on the benefit to employers: ‘is not the distinction between labour which produces capital and that which does not produce it the basis for an understanding of the process of capitalist production?’ (Marx and Engels 1975–2005, vol. 31, p. 190). He suggests that Smith’s disapproving attitude to labour that does not give rise to surplus value is typical of the rising bourgeoisie’s hostility to the older social system from which the ‘unproductive’ occupations have come.

> All these illustrious and time-honoured occupations—sovereign, judge, officer, priest, etc.,—with all the old ideological castes to which they give rise, their men of letters, their teachers and priests, are *from an economic standpoint* put on the same level as the swarm of their own lackeys and jesters maintained by the bourgeoisie and by idle wealth—the landed nobility and idle capitalists. They are mere servants of the public, just as the others are their servants. They live on the produce of other people’s industry, therefore they must be reduced to the smallest possible number (Marx and Engels 1975–2005, vol. 31, p. 197).

However, he goes on, once the bourgeoisie has gained control of the political apparatus, it is able to redefine the ‘ideological castes’ as serving its interests—and now the apologists for capitalism (often clergymen or university professors themselves, as Marx points out) turn about and defend these professions as being ‘productive’ after all.

So where does teaching fit within the occupations that provide services rather than contribute to the increase of capital? As we noted, Marx says that ‘education produces labour capacity’. In purely economic terms, it has much the same significance as medicine, in so far as that maintains or restores people’s ability to work.

> As to the purchase of such services as those which train labour capacity, maintain or modify it, etc., in a word, give it a specialised form or even only maintain it—thus for example the schoolmaster’s service, in so far as it is ‘industrially necessary’ or useful; the doctor’s service in so far as it maintains health and so conserves the source of all values, labour capacity itself, etc.—these are services which yield in return ‘a vendible commodity, etc.’ [citing Adam Smith’s expression], namely labour capacity itself, into whose costs of production or reproduction these services enter (Marx and Engels 1975–2005, vol. 31, pp. 22–23).

Yet Marx goes on to note that both the amount of new labour and its productivity may vary owing to circumstances, so that ‘the labour of the doctor and the schoolmaster does not directly create the fund out of which they are paid, although their labours enter into the production costs of the fund which creates all values whatsoever—namely, the production costs of labour-power'. Once again, then, these personal services are 'unproductive labour' according to Adam Smith's criterion—unless they are simply added on. 'Productive labour would therefore be such labour as produces commodities or directly produces, trains, develops, maintains or reproduces labour capacity itself' (Marx and Engels 1975–2005, vol. 31, p. 27). In that case, it is not so arbitrary to exclude the training that develops work skills.

The situation of education becomes clearer when we consider the capitalist and working classes as a whole. The labour of teachers then appears as an overhead expense. That is, it is necessary to keep the whole system going, but not identifiable as adding value directly to commodities. Production requires a lot of activities of this kind, and they may become full-time occupations. 'If by a division of labour a function, unproductive in itself although a necessary element of reproduction, is transformed from an incidental occupation of many into an exclusive occupation of a few, into their special business, the nature of this function itself is not changed' (Marx and Engels 1975–2005, vol. 36, p. 135). The examples Marx gives are salespeople, bookkeepers and messengers, but the point applies beyond the sphere of circulation. At the same time, there must be a strong imperative to keep these costs down to a minimum, since whatever revenue is spent on them means a reduction in the surplus value available for reinvestment as capital. This economic pressure will presumably apply to other occupations as well that lie outside the mechanism of profit-making capital. One of these is, of course, teaching.

The issue is not just about keeping costs (which here means wages) down. It is about what kind of work teachers are doing—and what kind of work they understand themselves as doing. One way to approach this is through the debate over whether teaching differs from ordinary wage labour in crucial ways expressed in concepts such as autonomy, responsibility and collegiality. The general label that is most often used for this distinct model of work is 'profession'. As we shall see, Marx has something to say on this subject.

5.5 Is Teaching a Professional Occupation?

Teaching and learning are not simply the same process seen from two sides. For one thing, a lot of our learning is not due to any teaching, but done on our own account. Conversely, and more to the point, even good teaching may or may not result in learning. What teachers are being paid for, whether by a private employer or the state, must be considered with this fact in mind. Payment by results is not always the rule for providers of services. Doctors are still paid if their patients die, lawyers if their clients go to prison, and ministers of religion if their flocks continue to sin (Marx and Engels 1975–2005, vol. 31, pp. 185 and 188). Similarly, one may add, teachers are paid even when their students fail to learn. Teaching may well bring about learning, but the phrase 'bring about' indicates that they are not the same thing, even if they do occur at the same time.

All this makes sense where outcomes are not simply brought about by direct acts. Barbers and bricklayers can be held strictly accountable for the results of their labour, but where circumstances and other people's behaviour enter into the overall process, the same level of expectation is unreasonable. At the same time, the practice of payment for services rather than outcomes means that there must be some other way of ensuring the quality of the work, since we know that it can be carried out more or less well. This need is a crucial factor in the establishment of a distinct category of occupations: the kind that we call *professions*. So, let us turn to the idea that teaching is a professional occupation—that is, a kind of work that differs from wage labour, not only when that produces material objects, but also when it provides services—and see whether Marx can help us with this issue.

Any overview of the professions starts with the division of labour. Certain kinds of work depend on a body of specialised knowledge and skill, which in turn is based on past and present disciplinary research. Practical know-how is not enough; the expertise required in these roles involves theoretical understanding as well. Gaining this academic knowledge requires a lengthy period of study, usually done nowadays at a university (also the location of ongoing research in the field) which has the authority to certify that the required standard of achievement has been attained. That is one side of this model. The other is professional practice, which for those in these roles involves a high degree of control over their daily work. Along with specialised knowledge comes a need to make decisions and accept responsibilities that is not borne by people in other jobs. Just for that reason, professionals are expected to observe high ethical standards.

One problem remains: how can those without the specialised knowledge in question be confident that the work is being done as well as possible? Here we come to the crucial move that turns the whole issue into a social and political one. The lay public needs to be safeguarded from those who either lack expertise or misuse the power it brings with it. In other words, most people do not have enough knowledge of the subject to make their own judgements, but may suffer severe consequences if things go wrong.

The solution offered by professionalism is for these occupations to be organised in a way that supports public confidence in their members. Certification becomes the basis for a monopoly of practice: only people with the proper qualifications are allowed by law to work in that occupation and to call themselves by its official title. Usually the state does not do this directly. It is professional bodies established by statute law that control admission to the occupation, monitor practice according to its own standards and deal with incompetents and wrongdoers. The confidence that the community has in the profession as a whole can then inform its dealings with individual professionals. In these situations, a combination of trust on one side and responsibility on the other is taken to be wiser and safer than the contractual relation of provider and consumer. At least, that is the premise on which the system is based. As with Marx's class analysis, the big picture tells the story. An implicit contract exists between the profession and the community, involving both autonomy and accountability.

However, what Marx and Engels say in the *Communist Manifesto* makes this account look irrelevant. They suggest that the special status of professions is a thing of the past.

> The bourgeoisie has stripped of its halo every occupation hitherto honoured and looked up to with reverent awe. It has converted the physician, the lawyer, the priest, the poet, the man of science, into its paid wage-labourers (Marx and Engels 1975–2005, vol. 6, p. 487).

In draft notes written about the same time, Marx expresses open satisfaction with this outcome. 'What a great advance it was', he writes, 'that the entire regiment of clerics, doctors, lawyers, etc., hence religion, law, etc., ceased to be judged by anything but their commercial value' (Marx and Engels 1975–2005, vol. 6, p. 436). As so often with Marx, we have to suspect irony, or at least ambiguity. He likes what he calls 'the rough cynical character of classical political economy' because its plain speaking can serve as a critique of existing conditions (Marx and Engels 1975–2005, vol. 31, p. 195). In contrast, the successors of Smith and Ricardo are mere apologists engaged in special pleading on behalf of an established capitalist system.

So perhaps Marx is just telling us the facts of life: rightly or wrongly, the professional model of work is an obsolete concept, thanks to the rationalising power of capitalism. What replaces it is a more traditional way of ensuring the quality of labour—that is, putting someone in charge of it. Under capitalism the worker is a wage labourer, subject to the authority of the employer, who in turn markets the service to consumers. In that case, the standard of the product is the proprietor's responsibility. This is what Marx and Engels mean when they assert that the former professional is now like any other wage labourer. For teachers the employer may be the state rather than a private school owner, but the same conditions of work apply.

That is not the last word, however. In passages like this, Marx is speaking of the period in which capitalism is winning power, not of the later time when 'Bourgeois society reproduces in its own form everything against which it had fought in feudal or absolutist form' (Marx and Engels 1975–2005, vol. 31, p. 30). It is this later capitalism that concerns us, his readers. So we need to ask: instead of simply doing away with the professions, does capitalism now reproduce them in its own form? If so, what does that form consist in, and can it be seen in the case of teaching?

Nowadays teaching has acquired many of the typical features of a profession, but questions remain. How much control do teachers have over their daily work? How do their organisations act to protect their pay and working conditions? Does the public have a high regard for teachers, compared with the older professions? It is often said that teaching is a borderline candidate for professional status, struggling to maintain its position in the face of problems and setbacks. There are good reasons for this. 'Schoolteachers, especially those in grammar and high schools, are the economic proletarians of the professions', C. Wright Mills wrote in his study of middle class America, *White Collar* (Mills 1956, p. 129). For one thing, he explained, there are a lot of them: 'These outlying servants of learning form the largest occupational group of the professional pyramid'. Because their training is not as lengthy as older professions, they are recruited from lower social groups—an echo of Marx's observation about education and social mobility. And finally, they work in an environment where routine and conformity tend to prevail. Hence, 'teachers are often less independent minds than low-paid employees'.

All this sounds like Marx's poor schoolmaster, working 'like a horse' in a 'teaching factory'. Dentists and accountants may have independent practices, but the teacher is an employee and therefore, as Marx argues, 'Whatever his pay, as a wage labourer he works part of his time for nothing' (Marx and Engels 1975–2005, vol. 36, p. 136).

Surely things cannot be quite so bad? After all, today's teachers have a tertiary education and an up-to-date perspective on curriculum and pedagogy that informs their classroom work. They are not likely to be relying on an equivalent of *Eves's Examiner* for lesson plans. Yet teachers' work is influenced by forces outside the school. Many of the pressures that they experience, both individually and collectively, are due to an economic and political environment that in recent decades has seen governments promoting policies that centre on a reaffirmation of Adam Smith's faith in the efficiency and fairness of the free market. Any monopoly of practice is inconsistent with free trade: hence, this aspect of professionalism is under threat. Neoliberals reject the paternalism that they see in the traditional model of professionalism, and would endorse Marx's dismissal of high regard for professionals as outdated sentimentalism.

Despite these challenges, the professional model has not disappeared. The twentieth century saw it not only reaffirmed but even extended to new occupational roles. With Marx's help, we can suggest two contrasting reasons for this fact. One is that, from a capitalist standpoint, an adapted version of professionalism has advantages over a straightforward employee model of labour. The seeming exchange of labour for wages under capitalism promotes a sense of personal responsibility in workers and develops what Marx calls 'general industriousness' (Marx and Engels 1975–2005, vol. 28, p. 250). The culture of professionalism places great store on just these qualities. Further, its ethical insistence on placing the interests of others first discourages the kinds of industrial action that trade unions take to defend the interests of their members. In Marxian language, this looks like a typical ideological mindset that not only presents a false picture of social reality but also acts to the disadvantage of those who adopt it and behave accordingly. It is not surprising to hear calls for teachers to abandon the professional concept altogether and to identify themselves with the traditional working class.

What is more, it will be said, this is what is happening, whether we approve or not. What Marx and Engels asserted in 1848 (maybe prematurely) is finally coming true: the deprofessionalisation of teaching, along with other professional occupations. As the capitalist mode of production extends its power throughout society, the replacement of individual occupations by places within organisational structures is paralleled in the provision of services. Nowadays many doctors work in hospitals or clinics, while lawyers work in large firms rather than individual practice. Teachers, of course, have always worked in institutions. But capitalism involves settings that leave individuals with little autonomy, give them only the responsibilities that match their place in an organisational hierarchy, and keep a close eye on their performance. Marx notes the loss of autonomy occurring with modern manufacture. In place of the independent craftsman, workers are assembled in a workshop or factory and placed under the authority of the employer. He writes:

> It can even be laid down as a general rule that the less authority presides over the division of labour inside society, the more the division of labour develops inside the workshop, and the more it is subjected there to the authority of a single person (Marx and Engels 1975–2005, vol. 6, p. 185).

Within an educational institution that is run like a business, competing with other establishments for customers, their position is that of an employee acting under orders from management.

The nature of the work itself alters under this same pressure. When teaching methods are 'directed' towards more practical purposes, as Marx puts it, they are likely to become standardised and simplified, following the precedent of the division of labour in manufacture and industry. This process is often referred to as 'deskilling', and yet that label misses the point. Skill may still be needed, but not *judgement*—that is, an ability to deal with the endless subtleties of different individual cases, for which standardised approaches will not work. Without that need, the basic case for professionalism fails to gain a foothold. Conversely, however, occupational groups such as teachers can find in the professional model a weapon for defending themselves against these tendencies and, in particular, opposing pressures for increased managerial control over their work.

There is a genuine basis for this resistance in occupations where the practitioner has an irreducible area of freedom. Once the classroom door is closed, the teacher has a largely free hand, at least in the short term. In fact, this is one thing that attracts people to teaching as a career: it enables them to feel they are achieving something as individuals in their daily work. The same goes for university academics who not only teach but engage in disciplinary research. A century ago, Thorstein Veblen wrote: 'No scholar or scientist can become an employee in respect of his scholarly or scientific work' (Veblen 1918). He argued that the introduction of business principles into university life, already under way at that time, would run up against an impassable barrier in the intellectual independence of researchers. That was arguably an optimistic view, and yet this is an ongoing campaign at every level of education. Marx's writing suggests that it is the business model that is deeply ideological, not the opposing view.

We can even take this response one step further. Where it is realised, professional work may be the best available example of what Marx calls 'free activity'—better than the often cited case of artistic creativity because of its directly social character, and just as appropriate in being 'not mere fun, mere amusement' but rather 'the most damnably difficult, demanding the most intense effort' (Marx and Engels 1975–2005, vol. 28, p. 530). With collegiality as its form of solidarity, it gives rise to a kind of democracy, even if professions tend at the same time to be quite hierarchical in terms of specialised expertise. Is this just an ideological camouflage, as Marxist writers such as Magali Sarfatti Larson (1977) have suggested? Educators who reflect on their own experience are unlikely to be as dismissive, despite the temptations of cynicism. But perhaps this is where Marx's assistance runs out, and we have to make our own decisions.

References

Desai, M. (2002). *Marx's revenge: The resurgence of capitalism and the death of statist socialism*. London: Verso.

Eagleton, T. (2011). *Why Marx was right*. New Haven-London: Yale University Press.

Larson, M. S. (1977). *The rise of professionalism: A sociological analysis*. Berkeley: University of California Press.

Marx, K. & Engels, F. (1975–2005). *Collected works* (Vols. 50). London: Lawrence and Wishart.

Mills, C. W. (1956). *White collar: The American middle classes*. New York: Oxford University Press.

Small, R. (2005). *Marx and education*. Aldershot: Ashgate.

Veblen, T. (1918). *The higher learning in America*. http://socserv.mcmaster.ca/econ/ugcm/3ll3/veblen/higher. Accessed 21 May 2013.

Lightning Source UK Ltd.
Milton Keynes UK
UKOW04f0337190614

233681UK00001B/60/P